W9-BWF-155

MARCHING ORDERS

A TACTICAL PLAN FOR CONVERTING
THE WORLD TO CHRIST

DAN McGUIRE

Catholic
Answers
Press

Imprimatur
Rev. Jay H. Peterson
Vicar General, Diocese of Great Falls-Billings

Nihil Obstat
Most Rev. Michael W. Warfel
Bishop, Diocese of Great Falls-Billings

Published by Catholic Answers, Inc.
2020 Gillespie Way
El Cajon, California 92020
1-888-291-8000 orders
619-387-0042 fax
catholic.com

Printed in the United States of America

Cover design by Devin Schadt
Interior design by Claudine Mansour Design

978-1-941663-40-0
978-1-941663-41-7 Kindle
978-1-941663-42-4 ePub

To the souls of all the faithful departed;
but two in particular who are in need of prayers.

Thanks to my wife Kristen and son Sean
for their help in editing and reviewing the content of this book.

CONTENTS

INTRODUCTION

Most everyone has heard of medieval knights in shining armor. Far fewer know that knighthood and chivalry were informed by Catholicism. The gospel ethics of charity, goodness, uprightness, fairness, and noble conduct were meant to transform the warrior into a force for good—as much as was possible for one whose reason for existence was to kill his fellow man. Actual knighthood was far different than the symbolic or honorific knighthood we think of today. Military conflict and war were part of the warp and weft of life in medieval times and affected the daily lives of most people.

I chose a military theme for this book fully aware of this difficulty. I did so in order to stress a present-day reality: as long as we inhabit this pilgrim life on Earth, we are engaged in spiritual combat.

Another reality is that the orders of knighthood (and ranks of the military) were and are male bastions; however, men are, sadly, significantly absent in the life of the Catholic Church today. Women far outnumber men in active participation at Mass and in the other sacraments. Aside from those ordained to ministry, most of the people active in the Church today are women. They serve as extraordinary ministers of holy Communion, catechists, sacristans, and lectors far more often than men do. In prayer groups, adult education, devotional societies, and the pro-life and social justice movements, women comprise the majority of members and leaders.

On one hand, this is a good thing. It allows them to become involved, exercise leadership, and foster good works in a manner that, in the past, had been mostly missing. On the other hand, it gives the impression that religious concerns and activities are for the ladies, and the males are left to the realm of televised sports and video games. This is an impression the culture is swift to embrace and foster.

This book is my own small effort to awaken that other half of the people of God and encourage them to shoulder their share of the burden. Men have been fed the idea that religion is all about feelings, what I call the "group hugs and bubble-gum" school of faith. To those men who went through CCD or Catholic school in the late sixties and early seventies, this likely sounds familiar. Talk about an inversion of reality!

The Feminization of Religion

How many times have you heard other men say, or even thought to yourself, that religion is feminine? After all, it's about warm, fuzzy feelings, and that's the wife's department. Men seek cold hard facts, empirical evidence, logic and reason, not sentiment. Let's face it, how manly can faith be when in order to be in charge you have to be celibate and wear a robe?

How did we get this way? How can a Church that in-spired saints like Augustine, Anselm, and Aquinas be about warm fuzzies instead of rigorous, reasoned thought? How did a Church that invented the university become a place devoid of fact, evidence, and examination? There was a time when the brightest minds in the world were concentrated in the Church and founded universities in Paris and Bologna. The-ology was considered the queen of the sciences. The suspicion with which many contemporary people view religion is a false view fostered by our popular culture.

How did a Church built on the blood of martyrs become a bunch of sissies? There was a time when the heroism and courage of martyrs were the stuff of songs. Men and women were hailed for having the courage and strength to be a Christian in the face of torture and death. Now if a man says he loves the Lord, his manhood is likely to be seen as deficient (professional athletes excepted).

There are feminine as well as masculine aspects to the Faith, and the true interior life embraces both. Both men and women must participate in the interior life, and each is more naturally responsive to different aspects. The male is more drawn to the active aspects: battle for self-mastery, spiritual combat, and even asceticism. The woman is more drawn to the abandonment of self, sometimes directly to God but often also to the needs of others. She is more naturally vulnerable and receptive. Each aspect is necessary, and we seem to be designed so that there is an aspect that appeals to our nature.

These natural tendencies or inclinations can assist people in their conversion by providing a ready entry to the interior life. In God's magnificent plan, his grace builds on the human nature already present and raises it to a higher level. He takes us at whatever level he finds us and raises us up. He wants to raise us eventually to himself in the divine adoption that makes us sons and daughters of God. When Sacred Scripture tells us we have been made sons of God, it means that, through Christ, we are given the ability to have a father-son relationship with God almighty. It is possible, and it is free; but it is not easy. It is a fight and must be understood as such. Note the words of Pope Paul VI:

> This kingdom and this salvation, which are the key words of Jesus Christ's evangelization, are available to every human being as grace and mercy, and yet at the same time each individual must gain them by force—they belong to the violent, says the Lord, through toil and suffering, through a life lived according to the gospel, through abne-

gation and the cross, through the spirit of the beatitudes. But above all each individual gains them through a total interior renewal which the gospel calls *metanoia*; it is a radical conversion, a profound change of mind and heart (*Evangelium Nuntiandi*).

Spiritual Combat

The primary spiritual combat of the twenty-first century is the battle against unbelief and apathy. The Church has been called to a New Evangelization; the response is spiritual combat. Evangelization in the modern world requires a proactive mindset. There are varied forces at work that turn people away from religious faith. Effective evangelization involves not only identifying and reducing these forces but engaging in an internal and external battle against them in your own life. For this reason, the military mindset can be of particular help in addressing the spiritual needs of twenty-first-century men. The spiritual life is a battle and must be approached as such.

This is a handbook for the New Evangelization. It is aimed at men, exhorting them to active participation in the Church Militant alongside their mothers, wives, and daughters. They need to serve in a manner fitting for men. The Church needs its men, and they need to answer the call to arms. All people are called to evangelize. This entails a personal conversion and spreading the good news of salvation through Jesus Christ. The word *gospel* means *good news*.

The Second Vatican Council spoke of a universal call to holiness (see *Lumen Gentium* 8). Being an evangelist on the path to sainthood is not a mission for only the ordained or professed religious. It is the mission given to everyone at baptism. The Council Fathers wanted every baptized person to realize he has been called to this mission and that everyone was needed to do their part. The "New Evangelization" called for by so many voices in the Church today is simply a continuation of the preaching of Jesus of Nazareth and Vatican II. Nothing has changed—except the urgency with which the call to arms has been sounded. Because I see this call as a part of what has traditionally been called spiritual combat, this book will follow the basic order of operations used in the military, comprising five main sections or *paragraphs*.

Organization and Approach

As a twenty-year infantry officer in the U.S. Marines and now a theologian, I find this approach a natural one. Since it may not be natural to most readers, I explain what an operations order is and how it functions and then apply it to the evangelical task at hand.

A military plan for conducting operations consists of five basic parts:

- Situation

- Mission

- Execution

- Administration and logistics

- Command and signal

Even when used at the small-unit level, these paragraphs are expanded as needed. With the possible exception of the "mission" statement, each section is considerably longer and more detailed than a paragraph. At the beginning of each paragraph you will find an explanation of that particular section of an operations order, as well as its meaning, context, and organization. Then I will show how that particular chapter or section applies to the spiritual combat operation that is evangelization.

Some might question, or even take offense, that an author would present evangelization using a military motif. Although this will be addressed in depth later, consider that the Bible uses combat motifs and language in several places, particularly in the Psalms. The idea of progress in Christian discipleship as spiritual combat is as old as the Church itself. Three hundred years of persecution at the hands of the Jews (initially) and the Romans (extensively) made the early Church hyperaware that she was engaged in conflict on three levels: personal, communal, and supernatural.

First is the battle within each Christian seeking to more perfectly imitate the life of Christ. The effects of original sin (lust and weakness) make knowing and following God's will—and our own natural good—a struggle. Second is the battle against the world. This has two aspects: against the temptation to find contentment in pastimes and playthings of this passing world; and the very real struggle against determined persecution. The third level is the supernatural battle over the fate of immortal souls. This final level, the most difficult to grasp, is what lies behind the first two. Our pilgrim life on Earth is about getting to heaven, and there are forces at work against that goal. Seeing this whole reality is one of the keys to success.

Head and Heart

In drawing this material together, I have used insights gained from teaching introductory theology courses to undergraduates, many of whom have no religious background. This experience has forced me (to attempt at least) to move from the basic concepts to material appropriate for college-level study in a short time. From both sets of experiences I have also learned that once people have a grasp of the basics, they are eager to move on to more serious theology. This book too will begin with some basic but essential concepts and eventually bring in the masters' perspectives.

Many people need a primer on the rational aspect of faith. It is not simply an affair of emotion or how one feels. Emotion and imagination are a part of the life of faith, but they are not primary. They are good inasmuch as they are part of our human nature and therefore gifts from God. They can strengthen and enhance faith, but they can also lead us astray. Humans are rational creatures, so reason must lead the way.

The head alone cannot be convinced; the heart must also be drawn in. The human heart is drawn by the encounter with Christ. That encounter can take place in sometimes unexpected ways. It is most often successful through the encounter with other people who have been converted. People need education, and the Faith needs defense; but at the core, people need to fall in love with Christ again. They will follow neither a teacher nor a program—they will follow a joyful, living witness. They will be swayed by encountering others who have taken the risk and discovered beauty and joy—and the peace that passes all understanding (Phil. 4:7).

I give considerable space to knowledge because man is the rational animal. He is a member of the animal kingdom, but what chiefly distinguishes him from all other members of that kingdom is the ability to reason. Knowledge is necessary but not sufficient. There are numerous difficulties or obstacles to be overcome. Some will resist because they are opposed to having certitude about religious matters. They understand, at least intuitively, that, once they are confronted by the truth, they have an obligation to act on that truth (see *Fides et Ratio* 25).

This can be unsettling, because there is comfort in not knowing. There was a reason the inhabitants of Plato's cave did not want to leave. Others, having imbibed the zeitgeist, will claim that there is no objective or binding truth. For them all is subjective. They cling not so much to their own "truth" as to the belief that there is no truth in any sense of the word that has been commonly understood.

"What Is Truth?"

Truth is subjective in the sense that it must be known by subject but not in the sense that it is dependent on that knowing for its meaning. Every truth a subject encounters is placed within a constellation of truths (or suspected truths) already known by the subject. But truth has objectivity independent of the knower, and this can be unsettling. The movement to, and embracing of, truth in this life is a fragile and uncertain journey. It is also dangerous, because the truth makes demands.

Then there are those who are unsure that we can know the truth of things, though they wish it were so. We live in an information age, but we have lost the ability to move from information to truth. It is an age that asks, like Pontius Pilate asked Jesus, "Truth? What is truth?"

Finally, there are those for whom only what can be proved by empirical science counts as true. For now I offer them the simple observation that the nature of science is to challenge and to disagree with scientific "truth." Many of the great discoveries in science have been made because one individual refused to accept his generation's received wisdom.

Much ink has been spilled over the past decade by the self-described "New Atheists"—Richard Dawkins, Sam Har-

ris, Christopher Hitchens, et al.—who attempt to demonstrate that faith is unreasonable. But these atheists fail to
engage the traditional arguments for the logic of religious
belief. In those rare instances when their ilk attempts to engage thinkers of the caliber of St. Aquinas or St. Augustine,
there seems to be an impasse of understanding. Due to a lack
of knowledge of philosophical and theological language and
concepts, these pundits fail to engage the actual arguments in
any meaningful way.

I do not think that engaging the classical arguments is of
interest to these men. Instead, I see them as careful observers
of the popular culture. They seem to understand that most
people have little time or inclination to engage in sustained
debate. I see their intent as simply to saturate the public discourse with a volume of information that fosters confusion—
and perhaps paralysis.

Although salutary work has been done in rebutting their
arguments point by point (and it is necessary work), this is
not the best response if one is seeking to advance the cause of
religious belief. The enemy has indeed dug a pit in the path
of the religious seeker, and many have fallen into it. The entire
point of this exchange has become the exchange itself.

Battle on the Field of Logic and Reason

My background in military strategy leads me to see this as
an asymmetrical attack. I'll define this term more fully later
on; for now it is where a force masks its objective by using
multiple unconventional means of attack simultaneously, all
ordered toward the same objective. The New Atheists have
sought by sheer volume to move adherents of Christianity into the atheists' preferred arena and to distract potential
adherents.

sion, to the peace that passes all understanding, we must make
sure we ourselves possess it.

Talk of peace may seem at odds with the theme of spiritual
combat. Are we not to walk with courage the path that God
sets before us and vanquish the foes he places in our path? Yes,
but not man's way: God's way. We must look to the Christ as
our exemplar. Although there are times for making whips and
overturning tables (see Matt. 21:12), they are rare.

Paradox is at work here. Just as he is a king who rules by
serving, we must be warriors who conquer by loving. There
must be a divine balance modeled on Christ. He did express
anger (John 17:17) and frustration (John 14:9), but the Gospels show these as departures from his primary focus on love
and self-sacrifice.

Following Christ our captain, we must have frequent recourse to spiritual renewal through prayer. How often in
Scripture do we see Jesus seeking solitude in prayer? He even
separated himself from his disciples in order to pray—to com-
mune with his Father in solitude. Only then does he return
to his mission. A country song popular in the mid-2000s
captured this image well. The song tells of soldiers who get
letters from home. After the warrior has this brief respite of
spending time in a more peaceful world, "he picks up his gun
and gets back to work" (John Michael Montgomery, "Letters
From Home"). This is the attitude the spiritual combatant
must have to be successful.

The Idea of Spiritual Combat

My introduction to this theme was *Life of Anthony* (or An-
tony) written by St. Athanasius. St. Anthony was the first of
the Desert Fathers who, inspired by a sermon on the Gospel
story of the rich young man (see Mark 10:17-31), left the

world and went to the solitude of the desert to serve God in contemplation.

In this oasis he was assaulted by demons so severely that those visiting him saw bruises and physical wounds on his body from actual combat. The physical combat was an outward manifestation (and response) to the spiritual fight he was engaged in against the devil. Again we see the pattern: the main fight is not outward and violent but inward and spiritual. The warrior for Christ must always keep in mind this simple truth. The actual battles will come, but if one is not prepared through training in personal holiness and ever deeper personal conversion, he will fail. Until the battle has been fought on the interior level, there is no hope of exterior victory.

My next—and perhaps best—encounter with this concept was Lorenzo Scupoli's *Spiritual Combat*. Much of the book is devoted to the interior battle and very little to the fight against the world. We must vanquish worldly desires and attitudes within us before they can be vanquished outside of us. Consider the book you're holding as a practical follow-up to Scupoli's masterwork. He shows the type of training one must undergo, and this book tells us what to do with it. At the same time, one must never lose sight of the need for continual training in the interior life—just as Jesus and St. Francis showed us.

Finally, this book is aimed at men. It is meant to awaken in them the fire that burned so brightly in their ancestors in the Faith. To today's men I say:"You too have been called to work in the vineyard; and far too many have either never heard or never heeded that call. Hear it now and get to work." These are your marching orders.

1

SITUATION

THE SITUATION PARAGRAPH DESCRIBES HOW THE
MISSION FITS INTO THE OVERALL STRATEGIC OR
OPERATIONAL PLAN. IT INCLUDES A DESCRIPTION
OF THE FRIENDLY HIGHER AND ADJACENT FORCES
(AND THEIR MISSIONS) AS WELL AS ANALYSIS OF
THE TERRAIN AND THE ENEMY.

What is the situation in which we who are called to engage in a New Evangelization using spiritual combat
find ourselves? In 1994, when Pope John Paul II promulgated
his apostolic letter *Tertio Millennio Adveniente* ("Towards the
Dawn of the Third Millennium"), he called for renewed evangelization aimed particularly at former or nominal Christians.
Although his primary concern was the state of the Catholic
Church in Europe, I will focus on the situation in the United
States.

OBJECTIVES

In many European countries, less than 10 percent of Catholics go to Sunday Mass. In the United States, only about
one-fourth of the 78.2 million Catholics attend Sunday Mass.
As the largest single religious group in the country, Catholics make up about 25 percent of the population, and lapsed
Catholics another 10 percent. There's no escaping the implication: large swaths of Catholics are not convinced enough of

the Faith's importance to give it weekly priority. Even if one were to quibble with the reliability of polling data, it seems clear that there is good reason to take the call for a New Evangelization seriously.

Strategic Objective: the New Evangelization

Polling data from the Pew Research Center bring to light another dynamic about religious adherence in the U.S. Some 28 percent of American citizens have changed religions at least once.[1] The low-intensity practice of the Faith among Catholics is mirrored in the demise of mainline Protestant churches. Still, there seem to be some interesting dynamics about religious adherence in the U.S. Some of these are affected by generational shifts, others by immigration.

G.K. Chesterton wrote that the U.S. was "a nation with the soul of a Church."[2] Alexis de Tocqueville found that religious faith was central to understanding the people and the nation.[3] On the other hand, there's the quote sometimes attributed to Mark Twain: "In the beginning, God made man in his image. And man has been trying to return the favor ever since." My experience as a professor of theology aligns more with Twain's unsourced quote than with either Chesterton or de Tocqueville. We seem to be a nation of people similar to the character Petronius in the novel *Quo Vadis?* by Henryk Sienkiewicz. On the verge of his conversion to Christianity, Marcus Vinicius (his nephew) asks Petronius why he resists the call of Christianity. Marcus knows his uncle is a wise man and has come to

1. http://religions.pewforum.org/reports.
2. Raymond T. bond, ed., *The Man Who Was Chesterton* (Garden City, NY: Image Books, 1960), 125.
3. Alexis de Tocqueville and Thomas Bender, *Democracy in America* (New York: Modern Library, 1981).

understand that the message of Christianity is true. Petronius replies (in part):

> No, by the son of Leto! I will not receive it; even if the truth and wisdom of gods and men were contained in it. That would require labor, and I have no fondness for labor. Labor demands self-denial, and I will not deny myself anything. With thy nature, which is like fire and boiling water, something like this may happen at any time. But I? I have my gems, my cameos, my vases, my Eunice. I do not believe in Olympus, but I arrange it on earth for myself; and I shall flourish till the arrows of the divine archer pierce me, or till Caesar commands me to open my veins.

Petronius has the gods of Olympus arranged just as he wants them. Although he may not actually believe in them, they are a comfort and—more importantly—under his control. I think this is the same theme as Twain's. Americans are religious so long as that religion is a source of comfort. Once a religion begins to make demands, many of our countrymen are quite willing modify the religion to lessen those demands. Increasing religious mobility and decline in church attendance are in my estimation due in no small measure to the demands of discipleship.

Tactical Objective: Holiness

At its heart, the New Evangelization is about winning souls, about conversion. Conversion to faith is a *strategic goal*, but it is not the *immediate objective*. In military terms, a strategic goal is an overall vision or end-state that motivates numerous different operations or activities. An immediate objective is the end of a specific, limited action that is only a step toward achieving the strategic goal. The objective for the modern Christian soldier is deeper conversion aimed at personal holiness. I intend to focus on the objective while keeping in mind the strategic goal that gives rise to it.

The Center of Gravity

There are two key points to keep in mind. The first is that any successful operation is dependent on a proper determination of the enemy's "center of gravity." This refers to that one key aspect of the enemy's strength that, if successfully attacked, will cause his downfall. I see the center of gravity for the New Evangelization as the reluctance to accept the demands of discipleship.

The notably American traits of independence and self-sufficiency have served our country well on many occasions in our history. But in the realm of discipleship, they are a disaster. One of life's little paradoxes is that a nation so motivated by religion would at the same time chafe at these demands. The word *religion*, after all, comes to us from the Latin *re+ligio*: literally, "things that bind." At its core, the nature of religion is to bind one to a certain way of life and action.

Certainly there is more to religion than a simple set of rules governing one's behavior. The man Jesus of Nazareth had harsh words for the religious leaders of his day who were obsessed with the following of rules.

Then said Jesus to the crowds and to his disciples, "The scribes and the Pharisees sit on Moses' seat: so practice and observe whatever they tell you, but not what they do; for they preach, but do not practice. They bind heavy burdens, hard to bear, and lay them on men's shoulders; but they themselves will not move them with their finger" (Matt. 23:1-4).

In this same passage one can see that Jesus did not see observation of the rules as the problem. "Sitting on the chair of Moses" refers to the authority of Moses. Because the Pharisees have a legitimate authority, Christ tells the people to obey them but not imitate them. The former is an ethics of doing, the latter is an ethics of being—and this is what he came to show people. He came not to do away with the Law but to fulfill and perfect it (Matt. 5:17-18). He wished to set a fire on the Earth (Luke 12:49) and knew it would break even the closest bonds of family (Luke 12:52-53). In his commission to the Twelve to go out and conduct the first evangelization, he says:

> So everyone who acknowledges me before men, I also will acknowledge before my Father who is in heaven; but whoever denies me before men, I also will deny before my Father who is in heaven. Do not think that I have come to bring peace on earth; I have not come to bring peace, but a sword. For I have come to set a man against his father, and a daughter against her mother, and a daughter-in-law against her mother-in-law; and a man's foes will be those of his own household. He who loves father or mother more than me is not worthy of me; and he who loves son or daughter more than me is not worthy of me; and he who does not take his cross and follow me is not worthy of me. He who finds his life will lose it, and he who loses his life for my sake will find it. He who receives you receives me, and he who receives me receives him who sent me (Matt. 10:32–40).

Religion, then, is not about rules—but also not without them. I see the center of gravity as a reaction to this aspect of the faith. Just as with reason, rules are necessary but not sufficient. The popular advertising slogan for Outback Steakhouse—no rules, just right—is catchy, but logically contradictory. What can "right" mean absent some standard of judgment?

Certainly this is not always the fully conscious reason for resistance to the gospel of Christ. In our "Terrain and Obstacle Analysis" we will examine some of the myriad reasons people might give for the reluctance to follow where Marcus Vinicius was prepared to go. If I am correct, what lies behind these reasons, or what gives them added import, is the fear of the demands of discipleship.

In this type of an endeavor there is a second crucial distinction to make. The goal we seek, either operationally or strategically, is primarily accomplished by the Holy Spirit working within the individual person. Even the most gifted and charismatic evangelist is limited to effecting those things he or she can effect. Another human person may contribute to the conversion (or reversion) to faith; but is utterly incapable of either causing or sustaining it. Only the Holy Spirit can stir the soul to love. He can make use of our best efforts as well as our worst ones. The mission of the evangelist today is to supply the efforts to the best of his ability and allow the Holy Spirit to do with those efforts what he will; for whom he will, and according to his own schedule.

FRIENDLY FORCES: WHO THEY ARE, WHAT THEY BRING TO THE FIGHT

This will be a cursory introduction; more information can be found in paragraph 5, "Command and Signal." As a part of assessing the situation, we must have an understanding of our own resources and allies. We begin with God himself. Not only is he our strongest force in this battle, all our other forces spring from him.

God: the Ultimate Higher Headquarters

God is eternal love. He is also unchanging. His activity now is the same as it has ever been; he seeks to draw all of creation to himself. More specifically, he seeks to enter into a relationship of love with every person he has created. This is because he created us for that very purpose.

For the New Evangelization as understood in the military motif, God is the overall or strategic commander-in-chief. He determines the objectives and assigns each of his subordinate commands tasks commensurate with their abilities. He is responsible for ensuring that each part of the plan is coordinated so that the ultimate goal is accomplished. This is a key to understanding our own role in the spiritual combat—either as individual warriors or as the pilgrim Church on Earth.

He is God and we are not: simple, yet so easy to forget. Ours is to accept the part of the plan entrusted to us and not to worry about the big picture. In his infinite wisdom, he has already determined what we (again, as individuals or as the entire Church) are capable of and has already assigned us a mission. He is responsible, often through other layers of command, for ensuring that we are adequately trained to accomplish this mission. Our task is threefold:

- To participate in the necessary training and develop the necessary skills

- To clearly understand the mission given to us

- To carry out the mission

Simple but, as we will see, not easy.

Perhaps a bit more of an introduction to our commander is

necessary in order to grasp our own role. In the Introduction I mentioned how, when faith is seen as an emotional affair, it is an inversion of reality. As we progress, we will see other instances of the phenomenon I call "cultural inversion." This is where what we have been told is the opposite of what really is. Some of this is simple human weakness, but some of it is also part of the disinformation campaign waged by the enemy.

God seeks to enter into a relationship of love with every person he has created. This is because he created us for that very purpose. This much is true, but it suffers from a lack of proper focus. In order to grasp who and what God is for us (*pro nobis*), it is necessary to begin with who and what God is in himself (*per se*). Only in this light does what he does *pro nobis* take on its full meaning.

As human beings, we are used to looking at things from our perspective; that is entirely natural—and to a certain degree unavoidable. What other perspective does one have immediate access to? But until that perspective is examined in light of the larger perspective in which it exists, a distorted picture cannot help but emerge.

God Is Paradox

Where to begin then? Considering God in himself, we begin with a paradox. God is simple. By this, I do not mean easy to understand; you will see he is anything but simple in this sense. Rather, he is simple in the sense that there are no "parts" in God. From our perspective, he is loving and merciful; all knowing and all powerful; totally other and closer to us than we are to ourselves. He is the Creator of all and present in everything he created. Yet in all this, he remains simple. What appear to us as different actions or attributes of God are simply the refraction that takes place as God reveals himself to us through the prism of our finite intellect. His essence is his existence. His mercy is his judgment. His love is his wrath. All the myriad things we see in God are simply how he appears to us.

Note that at this point I make no distinction between the divine Persons who make up the Christian God. In due time, I will draw attention to the personhood-specific works attributed to the Father, Son, and Holy Spirit. There is no need to do so at this point—and ultimately no necessity to do so at all. As St. Augustine pointed out, no member of the Trinity works or acts alone. In any activity attributed to God, all three divine Persons are working or active. Anything said about God applies to each divine Person in a manner appropriate to each.

Perhaps another analogy would be helpful. Think of the operation of vision in the human animal. We look and we see—simple. But what is actually occurring in this simple act? (In the analogy that follows, I am not seeking a precise description of the biological process. My point is to be sufficient enough so that the analogy works.) Light from a source falls upon an object. Certain wavelengths of this light are absorbed and others are reflected. Of those that are reflected, some enter the eye via the pupil. There, they fall upon the inner eye and are again reflected, refracted, and absorbed. These are transformed into electrochemical signals that travel along the optic nerve to the brain. In the brain, they are re-assembled into an image. We "see" with our intellect, using the organs of our eye, optic nerve, and brain. In everyday life, what we are cognizant of is that we look and we see—simple, but in reality complex.

So God is simple. How we perceive God is complex. Eastern Christian theology has long insisted that God, in his essence, is beyond knowing. This idea is not foreign to the

Western Church, but it has never received as much attention as our Eastern brothers give it. The predominant (and modern) point of view is a focus on "God with us" or the immanence of God. Although this approach has its benefits, it also comes at a price. He becomes too much like us—only better.

An anecdote about the late Cardinal Avery Dulles illustrates the problem. He was concelebrating Mass while on vacation, and in the church was a large felt banner that read, "God is other people." Dulles said that it was all he could do to resist the urge to change the banner to read: "God is other, people!" He is not simply one among us; he is *the* One.

The Mind of God

Even when we do not perceive God as our buddy, we still can misconceive the divine nature. This is because his self-revealing has taken place in a manner fit for our finite nature and according to that nature. If he revealed his essence as it exists in glory, we could not hope to understand or love him. So when we think of God's "personality," we are using a form of mental shorthand; it makes him accessible, but it also obscures.

As a theology student, I suffered through an academic phase in which learned theologians tried to analyze the mind of God (more precisely of Jesus of Nazareth) at a time when psychoanalysis was all the rage in academic circles. I have no intention of inflicting the same pain on my readers. Although there may have been insights gained from such an exercise, they were certainly few—I can remember none—and I surely found nothing that would compare to St. Thomas Aquinas or St. John of the Cross.

Having introduced God and claiming that love is the cause of all that exists, let's dig a little deeper with the aid of Frank Sheed. He considers that God created all that is out of love for his creatures (us) and in order that we might have cause to love him in return. God's own joy or happiness cannot be increased by anything outside himself. All creation is pure gift and meant to be a source of happiness and wonder that might spur us to love the Creator and as incentive to love him for himself. In the same way, a child's parents hope he loves not just the toy he receives for Christmas or a birthday but the grandmother who gave him the toy. Those who say nature is their Church and that it is better to worship God outside than in a building are not entirely correct, but they are at least informed by a right impulse.

Sheed also points out that God made everything that exists out of nothing but the force of his own love. The theological term for this is *creatio ex nihilio*: "creation from nothing." This gives a different view of the immanence of God from that addressed in the anecdote about Cardinal Dulles. If God were not involved with all of creation at every moment, it (and us) would have to rely on itself (or ourselves). As Sheed explains:

> This fact that God made us and all things of nothing by a sheer act of his will is not simply a fact of history, something that happened an immeasurably long time ago. We may very well think of it as something that happened, because it did happen. But it implies as its corollary something that is happening here and now, happening from instant to instant and of the most vital importance to us. Because we are made by God of nothing, then we cannot continue in existence unless God continuously holds us in existence. There is an emptiness at the very center of the being of all created things, which only God can fill; not an emptiness merely in the sense that it cannot be happy without God; but in the sense that it cannot be at all without him. God does not simply make us and leave us.

To return for a moment to the carpenter: he can make a table and leave it and the table will continue, none the worse
for his absence. But that, as we saw in chapter 1, is because
of the material he used, namely wood. Wood is so consti-
tuted that it will retain a shape given to it. Similarly, if God,
having made the universe, left it, the universe would have
to rely for its continuance in existence upon the material it
was made of: namely, nothing.[4]

Love Is Why There Is Anything

One of the perennial questions of philosophy, and more re-
cently a question taken up by both theoretical and practical
physics, is "Why is there anything?" Physicists may point to
the Higgs boson or to dark matter and dark energy, but the
Church answers: "Love." Not that love is the *physical* force of
creation; it is the *why* that explains the physical force. This is
one of the keys of the New Evangelization. Love is the reason
for everything. All people were made for love and have a need
to be loved. To frame the entire discussion within the sphere
of love must be central. If God is our most powerful ally and
he is love, then certainly love is our most powerful weapon.

This is the appropriate place to say a few words about the
nature of human love. Poets and songwriters tell us that love
is a many-splendored thing—an inexhaustible and indescribable mystery. To treat the subject of love itself would be another book of its own (one that philosopher Josef Pieper has
already written). I will focus on one particular point that must
be made clear.

Love is a human act, which means it is governed by both
the will and the intellect. Love is not a feeling; it is not "chick-

4. Frank Sheed, *Theology and Sanity* (San Francisco: Ignatius Press, 1993), 132.

en soup" for anything or anyone. Love between persons has at its core a common dedication to something held by both parties to be greater than either of them. It is for this greater common good that one is willing to sacrifice whatever may need to be sacrificed for the shared love to thrive. If human love is at least all of this, and ultimately indescribable, what is God's love like?

Love is the desire of the good for the beloved, even at the cost of one's own personal good. This is why what "love" looks like is the best shown by a crucifix bearing a broken Jesus. God so loved the world that he was willing to suffer for his beloved. In the New Evangelization we must live a self-sacrificial love. Just as soldiers are willing to die for the greater good of accomplishing the mission, those who answer the call to the New Evangelization must be willing to sacrifice to accomplish the mission given them by their higher headquarters.

Just as any parent knows, love for a child includes discipline as well as hugs; rebukes as well as praise. One of the other keys for the New Evangelization is getting this part right. When the Almighty God is presented only as offering group hugs and fuzzy feelings, something goes terribly wrong. As the psalmist notes: "O LORD, our God, you answered them; you were a forgiving God, though you punished their offenses" (Ps. 99:8).

One of the more damaging theological trends of the past few decades has been to present the loving God as offering a love which precludes anger, wrath, and punishment. The Just Judge has been replaced by the doting father. Once again, the dominant imagery of a human (and quite modern, western) love has replaced the image of God's love as revealed in Sacred Scripture and the saints. His Son stated that he had come to light a fire on the Earth and to break the bonds of family with the sword of his mouth (Rev. 19:15). The fear of God as mentioned by the prophet Isaiah has been replaced by "reverence and awe before God." This pop psychology view of God's love can lead many to reject any form of Divine discipline to the point of a rejection of God himself—or at least his Church.

I will return to this topic in the obstacle-breeching plan as it is one of the keys to the enemy's center of gravity. For now, we must turn to what type of ally we have in God.

The Nature of the Battle

So what kind of an ally is this loving God in the spiritual combat in which we are engaged? Quite simply, he is the chief, and only necessary protagonist. Cardinal Balthasar, reflecting on the Apocalypse of St. John—aka the book of Revelation— notes that the battle depicted there between the forces of God and those of evil is already won, but still being fought. The Lamb is always already slain and at the same time victorious. The battle rages, but he is serene. Balthasar continues to write that the cosmic battle between the forces of heaven and hell seem to come to a crescendo and then recede. For him, this pattern represents a key to the spiritual combat which must be clearly understood.

The battle between good and evil as depicted in the final book of Sacred Scripture operates on three levels simultaneously. It is a cosmic battle waged by supernatural being in the realm of eternity. It is also the battle between good and evil which is revealed in human history. Finally, it is the battle of personal discipleship. It is waged inside every person as they struggle to know and do the good, to follow the truth. These are not separate battles, nor are they simply modes of existence of a single battle.

This is asymmetrical warfare at its most sublime. Until one is able to see any particular part of the spiritual combat in which one is engaged through this interpretive lens; one is fighting the wrong fight. Or rather, it is the correct fight but because it is not understood, the plans and strategies employed are insufficient.

Returning to Cardinal Balthasar's thought, he notes that the battle—though still raging—is already won. Then why does it not look that way? Why must the battle be joined? Why is there a need for a New Evangelization and a spiritual combat? Can we not simply let events take their course and be confident in the final victory? No; the victorious Lamb can inspire a sure confidence, but not complacency. This is a paradox of the Christian faith, so the key to understanding it lies in the writings of St. Paul. In the beginning of his letter to the Church at Colossae he writes:

> Now I rejoice in my sufferings for your sake, and in my flesh I complete what is lacking in Christ's afflictions for the sake of his body, that is, the church, of which I became a minister according to the divine office which was given to me for you, to make the word of God fully known, the mystery hidden for ages and generations but now made manifest to his saints (Col. 1:24-26).

Though the final outcome of the battle is known, there is work yet to be accomplished. St. Paul can only claim that something is lacking in the suffering of Christ if that lack is there by design. The former Pharisee, well studied in Greco-Roman philosophy, surely understood that no action of God could be anything but perfect. He points to a "lack," something insufficient or missing in the Passion of the Christ. This lack can only be understood as a portion of the fight which is left to the Church *by design*. If believers are called to "put on Christ" (Gal. 3:27), then they must be prepared to take their part in his fight and be prepared to suffer as he suffered.

Take up your cross and follow me (see Matt. 16:24, Luke 9:23) means that in every age the battle between good and evil must be fought. Within the soul of each participant and on the stage of world history a part has been given us to play. This is what discipleship means: it is being continually formed into the image and likeness of Christ. This is the nature of conversion, the necessary and continuing task of the modern knight. It is at the same time his training and the chief weapon he wields against his foes. Much more will be said about this aspect, but it is time to get back to examining our allies and their missions.

Angels and Saints

We have other supernatural allies on our side: the angels and the saints. The angels are supernatural by nature, while the saints are so by grace. The saints, those who have gone before marked with the sign of grace, by grace, represent the goal of our conversion. They have been totally conformed to the will of God, while we are still a work in progress. The angels, supernatural by nature, have been conformed to the will of God at their creation. According to St. Thomas Aquinas, angels are given one instant of free will at their creation. Those who choose obedience to God remain with him. Those who opt for disobedience (i.e., for their own will) are what we call demons.

These allies can want nothing other than what God himself wants. Therefore, they desire and will work above all for the salvation of souls. They are our allies in that they will do whatever they are asked or tasked to do to secure God's objective. Only God can task them, but we can ask them—and should on a daily basis—for assistance.

Angels and saints have a natural affinity for us and our struggles. The saints do because they were once like us. Both have this affinity because they desire only what God desires for us. Although this may present a harmonious picture of our relationship with them; there is cause for setting such a view aside. Because they are totally conformed to God, they have a hatred of sin.

There is a reason why the angelic greeting in Sacred Scripture is "do not be afraid" (see Luke 1:13, 30). There must be something about their appearance that would lead to fear at being in the presence of God's messengers (and warriors). Because they are conformed to God, they take up the greeting that the Ancient of Days gave through the prophets and that Christ himself used many times. They do not inspire fear because they are supernatural beings (nor do they have Technicolor wings as depicted in the children's catechisms of decades past) but because they have a burning hatred of all things opposed to God. They are our allies so long as we are God's; they are our enemy to the extent we are not.

Sacred Scripture and Sacred Tradition

Our final nonhuman ally is the entire deposit of faith, and Sacred Scripture holds a preeminent place here. These books, written by men under the guidance of the Holy Spirit, contain all that God wanted to reveal about himself in written form. His fullest form of revelation (God's act of revealing himself) is contained in the person of Jesus of Nazareth, "the image of the invisible God" (Col. 1:15). In addition, we have been given the subset of revelation known as Sacred Scripture.

Catholics, Orthodox, and some Protestant denominations

understand that the Church has also received a teaching authority. From the Catholic perspective, this means that the
"deposit of faith" is contained in both Sacred Scripture and
in the Traditions of the Church handed down by the apostles.
As St. John the Evangelist writes:

> But there are also many other things which Jesus did; were
> every one of them to be written, I suppose that the world
> itself could not contain the books that would be written
> (John 21:25).

This deposit of faith is given to the Church to safeguard and
to use for instruction. St. Paul witnesses to this in his letter to
St. Timothy as he prepared to serve as bishop of one of the
communities founded by Paul:

> I am writing you about these matters, although I hope
> to visit you soon. But if I should be delayed, you should
> know how to behave in the household of God, which is
> the church of the living God, the pillar and foundation of
> truth (1 Tim. 3:14-15).

This is different from Christ's references to the traditions
which the Pharisees had added to the Law of Moses: "You
disregard God's commandment but cling to human tradition."
He went on to say, "How well you have set aside the commandment of God in order to uphold your tradition!" (Mark
7:8-9).

But is more like:

> May the Lord direct your hearts to the love of God and to
> the endurance of Christ. We instruct you, brothers, in the
> name of (our) Lord Jesus Christ, to shun any brother who

conducts himself in a disorderly way and not according to the tradition they received from us (2 Thess. 3:5-6).

Beloved, although I was making every effort to write to you about our common salvation, I now feel a need to write to encourage you to contend for the faith that was once for all handed down to the holy ones (Jude 1:3; see also all of the first chapter of 2 Peter).

It is a sad fact that the Church of Christ is divided by the competing manners in which these Scripture passages are interpreted. We can only pray that, at some point in God's grace, these divisions might be healed.

Apostolic Tradition: the First of Our Human Allies

Christ the Lord, in whom the entire revelation of the most high God is summed up, commanded the apostles to preach the gospel, which had been promised beforehand by the prophets, and which he fulfilled in his own person and promulgated with his own lips. In preaching the gospel, they were to communicate the gifts of God to all men. This gospel was to be the source of all saving truth and moral discipline (CCC 75).

In the apostolic preaching, one finds the "rule of faith" (*regula fidei*) that preceded the writing and compiling of the New Testament. The early Church was guided by the apostles, who had personal contact with and training by Jesus of Nazareth. They handed on their teaching to the bishops who took their place. To use a Star Wars analogy, the relationship between the apostle and the bishop (and subsequent bishops) was like the Jedi master and his Padawan learner. Years of close personal contact and teaching groomed the next person to take the master's place at the head of a local Church.

The Second Vatican Council's document on revelation (*Dei Verbum*) treats this matter most fully, but the *Catechism* sums it up:

> In keeping with the Lord's command, the gospel was handed on in two ways:
>
> —*orally* "by the apostles who handed on, by the spoken word of their preaching, by the example they gave, by the institutions they established, what they themselves had received—whether from the lips of Christ, from his way of life and his works, or whether they had learned it at the prompting of the Holy Spirit."
>
> —*in writing* "by those apostles and other men associated with the apostles who, under the inspiration of the same Holy Spirit, committed the message of salvation to writing" (CCC 75ff).

This revelation from God was meant to be a gift and guide for the rest of time. Accordingly, Jesus gives his apostles the power of the Spirit for the forgiveness of sins (see John 20:22). He builds his Church on St. Peter and gives him the keys to the kingdom of heaven (see Matt. 16:18-19). Since these mortal men would die, they in turn transferred their authority to the bishops who would replace them.

This transmission of the "deposit of faith" is a joint work of men and the Holy Spirit and is called Sacred Tradition. Because it is protected by the Holy Spirit, it can never be at odds with Scripture, which is also a work of the Holy Spirit. This is true even though fallible human beings have been given the task of teaching it to all nations (see Matt. 28:19-20).

Sacred Scripture and Sacred Tradition are means of encounter with God. The former is a gift of the Holy Spirit mediated through specific men. The latter is the gift of Christ mediated by a succession of men who are leaders of his Church. Both are intended as means of encounter with God himself, to lead all men and women to conversion.

Sacraments and Spiritual Directors

The sacraments are key parts of the training for one engaged in the spiritual combat. One can think of the sacraments of initiation as part of basic training, enabling one to become a soldier of God. The sacraments of states of life (holy orders and matrimony) are like occupational specialty training. In the military, occupational specialty training is what takes the basic soldier and makes him an infantryman, a pilot, or a tank crewman. They prepare one to perform a specific task in the overall force. Finally, the sacraments of healing (reconciliation and anointing of the sick) are the medical procedures performed on the wounded. The sacraments, instituted by Christ and administered by his Church, are means of receiving the grace (training) necessary to accomplish one's mission. Just as training is successful only to the degree that one puts forth the necessary effort to learn, the sacraments require the proper disposition on behalf of the one receiving them.

Any good form of training has been tested and proved successful for imparting the skills or knowledge necessary. The sacraments are "efficacious": they contain within themselves that which is sufficient to bring about what they intend. But, like any form of training, they can fail. Both training and the sacraments depend on the trainee (or recipient of the sacrament). Unless the individual intends what the Church intends and freely cooperates with the graces he receives, the effect will be minimal—or for naught.

Another similarity between the sacraments and a good training plan is that their celebration (application) has changed over time, while the core aim or goal has remained the same. Any good training plan is constantly refined and updated to be properly suited to its goal and to the trainee. Although the nature of the sacrament cannot be changed—they are God-given and therefore already perfected in themselves—the rituals used to celebrate them can change and have changed over time. These changes have taken place to make more clear what the Church intends in administering the sacrament. They have also changed to better suit the candidates and foster in them the necessary cooperation.

Christian Anthropology

With all this divine assistance at our disposal and with the final victory assured, what need have we to consider any further friendly forces? The sad story of our human nature answers that question. As St. Paul pointed out, work has been left behind for the Church to accomplish. This essential work must be done, but the agents of that work are frail. Just as the angels can be either ally or foe, we can be our own enemy as well. This final section of paragraph one "Situation" will be a bit detailed but is absolutely necessary.

Anthropology comes to us from the Greek word *anthropos* ("human" or "man"). A Christian anthropology, then, is how we understand what the human person is. This encompasses both what the majority of people are like at any given time *and* what we are supposed to be like.

From a religious perspective, we begin with the book of Genesis where we find that man was made in the "image and likeness" of God (Gen. 1:26-27). This does not refer to any physical resemblance—we are bodily creatures and God has no body. Rather, it refers to our nature and abilities. Of course, one does not get very far into Genesis when one encounters the story of the Fall—Adam, Eve, and the forbidden fruit.

So man is both the image of God *and* a fallen creature. Humans are at the top of the order of being among all earthly creatures; but they are also wounded and broken things. In order to get the most out of them (and us) in our spiritual combat, we need to better understand them. Since I have mentioned that we begin with Genesis, a word of caution is necessary. There is no need to see Adam and Eve as the first two people who ever existed and understand that all humans are their offspring. Modern genetics shows that this is almost certainly impossible; but it also shows that "[t]he proportion of human genetic variation due to differences between populations is modest, and individuals from different populations can be genetically more similar than individuals from the same population."[5]

As the modern study of genetics unfolds, it seems every answer dashes previous assumptions and raises more questions. It is safe to allow geneticists to figure all that out, because it is beside the point. The book of Genesis is not intended as a historical account of the beginning of the human race. The text itself tells us not to read it as such. When Cain is banished by God for killing his brother Abel, his concern is that the other people will want to kill him (see Gen. 4:12-17). The story simply assumes that other people are nearby and had been for some time.

---

5. *Genetics*, 2007 May; 176(1): 351–359. "Genetic Similarities Within and Between Human Populations"; D.J. Witherspoon, S. Wooding, A.R. Rogers, E.E. Marchani, W.S. Watkins, M.A. Batzer, and L.B. Jorde.

The stories in Genesis are meant not as history but as mythology. They attempt to tell a complex story using images to convey an underlying truth. The truth is that man is of an entirely higher order than all other animals; he is meant for communion with God, but by his own freely chosen actions that communion has been broken, and as a result he suffers in his very nature.

Of course, Genesis is not the only place one encounters stories that seek to address what is wrong with the human person. Nearly all world religions and primitive philosophies have some form of dealing with the problem of man. In its simplest form, it is a recognition that man is generally ordered (or directed or desirous) of the "good" and at the same time capable of great evil. In fact, most of the world's great literature and drama are based on this same incongruity. Understanding how Anakin became Lord Vader is an exercise in understanding how our weakened nature is subject to the lure of power and evil. We care because it is the story of mankind and the dangers that lurk within us.

So one can base these questions on any number of sources, but in the end the same questions remain: who or what are we, what went wrong, and can it be remedied? Obviously, I choose to rely on a religiously motivated bias in understanding the human person, but not a strictly religious one. Wherever a ray of truth can be found—be it in philosophy, genetics, biology, or psychology—it is welcome if it helps us understand the human person.

The Analogy of Being

So we begin with the positive: the image and likeness of God. I see image and likeness as referring to the capabilities of the human person that make us little less than a God (see Ps. 8:5).

In order to begin here, I need to introduce something theologians refer to as the "analogy of being." This is a term used to describe the fact that there are certain qualities we share with God, the source of all being. Because we can understand to some degree how these qualities operate in us, we can gain insight into how these qualities operate in God.

Although for every similarity there is a greater dissimilarity—since he is God and we are not—we can get some idea about *him* by looking at *us*. Conversely, if we want to understand the best we can be, the model and exemplar of our capabilities is how close they come to the manner in which we see those capabilities effective in God. Psalm 8 aside, we are a good deal less than God, but the similarities remain and give us insight.

Many capabilities or attributes could be chosen, but we will begin with the three primary ones of intellect, love, and creativity. Man stands alone among all animals in his intellectual capabilities. Certainly there are other intelligent animals. Use of tools and language/communication are common indications of intelligence among animals. But there is both a quantitative and qualitative difference between the capabilities of the human intellect and those of lower-order animals—even other primates and cetaceans (dolphins and whales). Given a thousand years and a thousand word processors, monkeys would not produce a Shakespearean sonnet. Intelligence sets us apart from other members of the animal kingdom and moves us closer on the scale of being to angels and God.

Of course, there are many things about how our intellect works that we still do not know. Take something as simple as a thought: what exactly is a thought, and how does it work? For that matter, what is consciousness itself? Again, modern science has made great strides in understanding but is still unable to describe (or at least agree on) such basic questions as these. At a minimum we can say two important things. First, that our intellectual capacity is nearly unlimited; second, that the human person is a question asker.

On the nearly unlimited nature of the intellect, one need only consider the history of man's intellectual achievement. We no longer live in a world where people were sacrificed to appease the sun god to end an eclipse, nor are we under the impression that the Earth is at the center of the universe. We live in an age where the entire human genome has been mapped, and spacecraft wander the solar system and the surface of Mars, sending back data for further study. There seems to be no limit to what the human intellect will discover. Particularly since the dawn of the scientific revolution, we seem to be coming ever closer to the idea the Psalmist gave voice to so long ago.

> When I look at thy heavens, the work of thy fingers, the moon and the stars which thou hast established; what is man that thou art mindful of him, and the son of man that thou dost care for him? Yet thou hast made him little less than God, and dost crown him with glory and honor (Ps. 8:3-5).

Thomas Aquinas saw this clearly. He wrote that the world is made up of "divine intelligibles." All things in the order of creation were divine in the sense that they were created and held in being by God. They were intelligible because they could be understood by us. The science of St. Thomas's day was rudimentary at best, but the point he sought to make was that, because our intellect was similar to the Creator's, all things could potentially be known to us. This was not a scientific argument, but a philosophical one. Because there was a relationship between the creative intellect of God and the finite intellect of man, there was no reason that we could not come to understand all that had been created.

This is a distinction between the secular study of anthropology and Christian anthropology. Secular anthropology explains what it sees and reasons to how it developed as it did, and (perhaps) toward what end. Christian anthropology asks why it is the way it is. Along with philosophy, it asks things like: Who is man? What is the purpose of life? Where are we going? How then should we live?

Creation and Beauty

There is a further interesting aspect of our intellect that distinguishes us from other animals. We can create things for no practical purpose. When a chimp uses a stick to get ants from an anthill, it is a tool with an end: nutrition. When the bird learns to drop the clam onto the parking lot pavement so that it breaks open, it also seeks nutrition as an end. Animals teach their young how to hunt or defeat a predator. All of these intelligent activities have an end or goal in sight.

Only the human can create things with no practical end— we call this "art." What we consider one of the highest achievements of man serves no practical purpose save to demonstrate either what is possible or what is beautiful (or both).

There seems to be another innate desire in man: the desire for beauty. Some of the greatest (and most tragic) works of art have been in response to this desire, which man alone seems to possess. We will return to the idea of beauty as we examine conversion, but at this point it is enough to establish that it is a motivating factor behind the human intellectual achievement.

All of these observations about the human person are wonderful to behold. We have capabilities and powers that set us apart from the rest of the animal kingdom, but we also have unique problems and weaknesses. As I mentioned above, only the human animal ponders and rebels against his own mortality. Mary Shelley's *Frankenstein* was an extended literary examination of the problems this can lead to. More pressing is the problem of human evil.

Observers of man from almost all disciplines are in agreement that man is oriented toward and desirous of the good; and simultaneously capable of great evil. The search for the answer to this riddle has gone on for millennia. The problem is compounded by the fact that man is not only a riddle—a thing he himself does not fully understand—but he is also a sphinx; he provides no suitable answer for himself.

The Riddle of Human Evil

Beginning with the ancient Greeks, and for most of human history, the search for an answer to the riddle of human evil has been found in God (or the gods). For Christians, the answer is original sin and the fall from grace. Oriental mysticism answers that there is evil in the world because the material world is separated from the One. The One is a spiritual entity that is all good, and evil is the result of being composed of matter. A person (if he is devout) must undergo a succession of lives, each being "higher" than the last, until finally he is released from his bondage in the material world and is united to the One in a spiritual realm.

Evil exists only in the material world from which we need to escape. Pagan pantheism offered that the gods inflict suffering and evil on people out of jealousy and bickering among themselves. Humans are largely unintended recipients of evil—though in some cases the gods inflict evil on a person out of spite or jealousy toward a person who has become a challenge to them or has not shown enough respect. Because it is willed by the gods, it is evil only from our perspective.

Finally, secular humanism answers that God does not exist and man is, by nature, a competitive and vindictive animal. Life is "nasty, brutish, and short,"[6] and the ones who will survive and prosper must do so to the detriment of the weak. Evil and suffering are built into human existence, just as in the rest of the animal kingdom. Certainly there are ranges of answers besides those outlined above, but the point is that every religion or system of thought has not only recognized this problem, but saw that it needed an explanation.

Returning to our Christian perspective, consider St. Paul. His letter to the Church at Rome was intended as his "calling card," or personal introduction, to that community. Much of the letter is concerned with the evil acts of men and how nothing can save them from evil except the grace of Christ. It is fascinating to see that, in this letter, he is quite frank about his own personal shortcomings:

> We know that the law is spiritual; but I am carnal, sold under sin. I do not understand my own actions. For I do not do what I want, but I do the very thing I hate. Now if I do what I do not want, I agree that the law is good. So then it is no longer I that do it, but sin which dwells within me. For I know that nothing good dwells within me, that is, in my flesh. I can will what is right, but I cannot do it. For I do not do the good I want, but the evil I do not want is what I do. Now if I do what I do not want, it is no longer I that do it, but sin which dwells within me. So I find it to be a law that when I want to do right, evil lies close at hand. For I delight in the law of God, in my inmost self, but I see in my members another law at war with the law

6. Thomas Hobbes, *Leviathan*, ch. 8.

of my mind and making me captive to the law of sin which dwells in my members. Wretched man that I am! Who will deliver me from this body of death? (Rom. 7:14-24).

In his letter to the troublesome Church at Corinth, he was equally forthcoming:

And to keep me from being too elated by the abundance of revelations, a thorn was given me in the flesh, a messenger of Satan, to harass me, to keep me from being too elated. Three times I besought the Lord about this, that it should leave me; but he said to me, "My grace is sufficient for you, for my power is made perfect in weakness." I will all the more gladly boast of my weaknesses, that the power of Christ may rest upon me (2 Cor. 12:7-9).

This, then, is the situation of our earthly allies. We are all prone to sin and weakness; only the grace of Christ gives us hope that we will one day be set free. More significantly, we are always already under attack by the enemy. St. Matthew showed, in his Gospel, how the Church was under attack from the moment it was revealed. All those who seek a position in the line of battle must understand that the warfare has begun long before they answered the call to take up arms. Even those who shrink from the fight are nonetheless already engaged.

But the same St. Paul, in spite of all his problems, saw that there was work to be done and that he was (and we are) the ones required to do it. On the one hand, we are little less than gods; on the other, we are slaves to sin. These are our (earthly) allies, and the battle has been joined.

INTELLIGENCE

Having surveyed the situation and friendly forces, we now turn to the enemy. In this section we must identify the enemy and assess his capabilities. Then we try to think of his most probable course of action and his most dangerous course of action. Without a clear picture of the forces arrayed against us, we cannot hope to succeed. It is a truism that no plan survives first contact with the enemy; sometimes it does not survive intact on first exposure to friendly forces, either. But if our plan is sound, we are focused on the mission and know the general situation; we can adjust on the fly.

Identify the Enemy

There are multiple forces arrayed against the New Evangelization. Some are human (either complicit or unintentional) and some are institutional. The law of unintended consequences dictates that there are times when the very institutions we seek to use in our cause may work against us. Once we are clear on what we face, we can determine the best approach. This will be most complex when dealing with the human forces whose motivation to resist or impede conversion to faith may not be fully known even to them.

I start with the oldest and most dangerous enemy: Satan, the devil, the Prince of Lies. St. Peter warns us about him in his first letter; "Be sober, be watchful. Your adversary the devil prowls around like a roaring lion, seeking someone to devour" (1 Pet. 5:8). That same warning continues today from his successor, the current Bishop of Rome. Pope Francis made the devil a central theme of his preaching in the early months of his pontificate. Perhaps he sees that this particular adversary has been too long neglected. Ask yourself: when was the last time you heard the devil mentioned in a homily? Perhaps he is seen as passé. It seems to strike many people as superstitious to call to mind that there are supernatural forces at work in the world.

In the beginning, it was not so. Scripture is full of warnings about the activity of the devil. In the Old Testament, he takes a leading role in both Genesis and Job. He is also found in the Torah (Lev. 16:26), the prophets (Isa. 14:12-22, Ezek. 28:12-19, and Zech. 3:1-2), the wisdom literature (Ps. 109:6); and in the historical books (1 Chron. 21:1). There are some who claim there is little mention of the devil in the Old Testament, but this is not quite true. What is true is that he goes by a variety of names. This is not surprising, given that the human authors came from a wide array of tribes, kingdoms, and eras; each had its own way of referring to the forces of evil. He was the Evil One, the Adversary, Azazel, Beelzebub, the Serpent. He came in a variety of disguises—even as an angel of light, as the name Lucifer would imply ("light bearer" or similar; see Isa. 14:12).

The ancient Israelites knew well who the enemy was. In the New Testament, the references to Satan and his activity are multiplied by a factor of (at least) four. Whether one looks at the Gospels or the Letters, the Evil One is always seen as actively opposing the activity of Christ and his Church. In addition to Peter's letter cited above, I want to focus on one critical set of Gospel passages. In Matthew's Gospel, two stories—placed one after the other—are crucial to understanding the role of the devil as understood in the early Church.

St. Peter's confession of faith and designation as the Vicar of Christ is well known:

Now when Jesus came into the district of Caesarea Philippi, he asked his disciples, "Who do men say that the Son of man is?" And they said, "Some say John the Baptist, others say Elijah, and others Jeremiah or one of the prophets." He said to them, "But who do you say that I am?" Simon Peter replied, "You are the Christ, the Son of the living God." And Jesus answered him, "Blessed are you, Simon Bar-Jona! For flesh and blood has not revealed this to you, but my Father who is in heaven. And I tell you, you are Peter, and on this rock I will build my church, and the powers of death shall not prevail against it. I will give you the keys of the kingdom of heaven, and whatever you bind on earth shall be bound in heaven, and whatever you loose on earth shall be loosed in heaven" (Matt 16:13-19).

This passage is immediately followed by an equally famous passage, and the placement is not by chance. Continuing on, one reads:

From that time Jesus began to show his disciples that he must go to Jerusalem and suffer many things from the elders and chief priests and scribes, and be killed, and on the third day be raised. And Peter took him and began to rebuke him, saying, "God forbid, Lord! This shall never happen to you." But he turned and said to Peter, "Get behind me, Satan! You are a hindrance to me; for you are not on the side of God, but of men" (Matt. 16:21-23).

Awareness of Satan

What Matthew, and through him the Holy Spirit, is trying to tell us is that from the moment the Church is revealed (in the person of Peter), it was—and always will be—under attack by Satan. Jesus knew that Peter's earlier words—"Thou art Christ, the Son of the living God"—were under the inspiration of his Father. He also understood the subsequent words "this shall not be" were inspired by the devil. His reply "Get behind me, Satan" is aimed not at Peter but at the real enemy. Just as the Christ knew who he had to fight, so do we. Unfortunately, just as Peter was not aware of how the evil one was acting in him, we are often unaware of how he may be influencing us.

To make clear that this was a fight that would not end until the Second Coming, Jesus ends the dialogue with a warning:

> Then Jesus said to his disciples: "If any man will come after me, let him deny himself, and take up his cross, and follow me. For he that will save his life, shall lose it: and he that shall lose his life for my sake, shall find it" (Matt. 16:24-25).

In the writings of the early Church Fathers, the Evil One plays a central role. Be it the Desert Fathers, Athanasius's *Life of Anthony*, or any number of other treasures of the first six centuries, one finds constant references to the activity of the devil and the warning to be on guard. This trend continued through the Middle Ages, particularly in the spiritual guides still so popular today. The reason people keep reading books like Thomas à Kempis's *Imitation of Christ* or Scupoli's *Spiritual Combat* is that they contain wisdom often absent in our day. Prior to the elevation of Francis to the papacy, this kind of talk had been marginalized. We would do well to follow the lead of the leader of the Church and take seriously what has been neglected. If we do not know whom we fight, how can we hope to prevail? Worse yet, if we do not acknowledge we are in a fight, we cannot help but be defeated.

Satan is still referred to by multiple titles. He is called, among other things, the "Prince of Lies," the Accuser, the Adversary, and the "ruler of this world." He continues to appear in a variety of disguises. And so he must, for if he showed his true countenance, who would do his bidding? Although the focus on the constant activity of Satan as the Adversary has waned, it is no less important now than it was to the Fathers and the inspired writers of Scripture. It may be that Pope Francis will have reawakened interest in this theme, but that remains to be seen. But if our approach is to be successful, we must be clear on exactly whom we fight.

Many will object to my emphasis on the diabolical and how well-intentioned people can be the devil's unwitting accomplices. They will react to any mention of the Evil One as an attempt to reduce the argument to "the devil made me do it." This is evidence that they too have missed the picture. When any mention of devil is reduced only to the devil, it is proof that the evil plan is actually working. As C.S. Lewis so succinctly stated (through his fictional devil-tempter Screwtape): first convince them we do not exist.

Original Sin and Its Effects

One of the first acts of the enemy resulted in what we call original sin. So we have an external enemy as well as an internal one. This is another aspect of asymmetrical warfare. St. Paul recognizes the effects of this sin as a deformity of human nature itself. In his letter to the Church at Rome, he offers his understanding of original sin:

> [A]s sin came into the world through one man and death through sin, and so death spread to all men because all men sinned—sin indeed was in the world before the law was given, but sin is not counted where there is no law. Yet death reigned from Adam to Moses, even over those whose sins were not like the transgression of Adam, who was a

type of the one who was to come. But the free gift is not like the trespass. For if many died through one man's trespass, much more have the grace of God and the free gift in the grace of that one man Jesus Christ abounded for many. And the free gift is not like the effect of that one man's sin. For the judgment following one trespass brought condemnation, but the free gift following many trespasses brings justification. If, because of one man's trespass, death reigned through that one man, much more will those who receive the abundance of grace and the free gift of righteousness reign in life through the one man Jesus Christ. Then as one man's trespass led to condemnation for all men, so one man's act of righteousness leads to acquittal and life for all men (Rom. 5:6ff).

Like the devil, original sin has been neglected in the preaching one hears on a given Sunday. So, if we want to know the enemy we face, it is necessary to spend some time revisiting this lesson once learned in the religious education of our youth.

We were created good, but something went horribly wrong. Much of the philosophy, drama, poetry, and literature of the world before the contemporary era wrestled with the idea that humans are odd animals. People are generally oriented toward the good but are also capable of great evil. What explains this dual nature within us? Every culture and every religion has tried to answer this question. For Christianity, the answer is original sin. This sin explains why we struggle to know and do the good—and why ultimately we need salvation.

The story begins in the book of Genesis: with Adam, Eve, the tree, and the serpent. This is an allegory—an attempt to describe something using figurative language. Adam and Eve represent humanity before sin, and the serpent is the devil.

The fruit of the tree of knowledge of good and evil (never identified as an apple—that was from artistic renditions) signifies a grasping for power. Rather than rely on God's definition of good and evil, people wanted the ability (knowledge) to decide for themselves. The first sin was man's refusal to accept God's definition and the desire to substitute his own. The result was disastrous.

If one examines the biblical story closely, particularly the punishments that result, one can see the four disruptions resulting from sin.

- *Between man and God.* By breaking the only law they were given, Adam and Eve could no longer walk in the Garden with God but were fearful of him (see Gen. 3:10).

- *Between man and woman.* When confronted by God, Adam blames both God and Eve. "That woman *you* put here, *she* gave it to me." A far cry from "At last! This is flesh of my flesh and bone of my bone." Original unity between Adam and Eve is now replaced by fear and domination. Before their sin, they were naked without shame; afterward, they donned fig leaves to shield their nakedness from each other. They each perceive the other as a threat that must be guarded against—lust has damaged the sexual drive. The woman will still desire her husband, but rather than respond with love, he will dominate her (see Gen. 3:16). By extension, this enmity between Adam and Eve will serve as the basis for enmity between all people, though the primary and lasting damage is between the sexes, specifically in regard to human sexuality.

- *Between man and nature.* "Cursed is the ground because of you . . . it will bring forth thorns and thistles" (Gen.

3:17-18). Now even daily sustenance—freely given in the Garden—becomes a labor. What once had been effortless becomes a struggle.

• *Within man himself.* Being cast out of the Garden represents being left to deal with the consequences of one's deciding for oneself. What we find is that knowing and doing the good—which we still desire—is no longer effortless. Life has become a struggle, because we got what we reached for.

Evangelization Requires Conversion

Although St. Augustine may have been the first one to develop a systematic understanding of the concept of original sin and the consequences of the fall from grace, he was far from the first to notice the problem. Christ spoke of it during his public ministry. He was keenly aware of his own disciples' inability to break free from their weakness and to follow him as they desired. Of course, the apostles were not the cream of Israelite society. Humble fishermen neither possess well-trained minds nor are gifted administrators.

I sometimes wonder if during those times when he went off alone to pray to his Father, it might have gone something like this: "Father, do you really expect me to build my Church on these men? I have always trusted you, but a bunch of fishermen? Not really the best the Chosen People has to offer, are they? Nevertheless, thy will be done." But the apostles, who would go on to accomplish so much through God's grace, serve as perfect examples of human double weakness: our finite nature and its weakness (deformation) due to sin. Man no longer can easily and readily know the good; and even once he discovers it, he has difficulty following it.

Jesus dealt with his disciples' inability to understand what he was trying to teach them (see Luke 9:45). Even when he explained things to them in detail after speaking to the crowds in parables, they were slow to grasp his meaning (see Matt. 13:10-17, 13:36-43). All four Gospels show us Jesus as the traditional Jewish rabbi. He was a man of wisdom who gathered to himself a small group of men for instruction. They traveled with him and learned from him on a daily basis.

But each of the Gospels gives a slightly different perspective on this time of preparation for the future leaders of the Church. Matthew's version shows us the patient teacher. Mark and Luke show us the reason for such patience, as they tend to highlight what poor students he had. John even shows his frustration at their lack of understanding when, after the Last Supper, Thomas and Phillip asks Jesus questions that seem to indicate they still don't get it:

> Thomas said to him, "Lord, we do not know where you are going; how can we know the way?" Jesus said to him, "I am the way, and the truth, and the life; no one comes to the Father, but by me. If you had known me, you would have known my Father also; henceforth you know him and have seen him." Philip said to him, "Lord, show us the Father, and we shall be satisfied." Jesus said to him, "Have I been with you so long, and yet you do not know me, Philip? He who has seen me has seen the Father; how can you say, 'Show us the Father'?" (John 14:5-9).

During his public ministry, Jesus had to answer their desire for reward after giving up everything to follow him (see Mark 10:28, Matt. 19:27). He tolerated their petty jealousy (see Mark 9:38-39) and their desire for privileges of rank and recognition (see Mark 10:37, Matt. 20:21—though Matthew places the request as coming from the mother of the sons of Zebedee rather than the sons themselves). He suffered their well-meant attempts to keep the rabble from pressing in on him (see Mark 10:47; Luke 8:45, 18:38). In all of this, we can see how even those closest to him were unable to grasp what he was trying to teach them. Those devout Jews were still suffering the effects of original sin, which blinds a person and renders him unable to know or do the good without the aid of grace.

The apostles, then, were the first to be in need of not only evangelization but of an ongoing and ever-deeper process of conversion. Even they needed continually to discover new depths to their faith. While they responded immediately to Jesus' initial call, their time of preparation was an ever-deeper entry into the mystery of their Teacher. It was not until they received the Holy Spirit at Pentecost that they were finally able to step out onto the rooftops of Jerusalem and proclaim the good news to others.

The first action required of the crowd after the first evangelization by members of the Church on Earth was conversion.

> Now when they heard this, they were pricked in their heart, and said unto Peter and the rest of the apostles, Brethren, what shall we do? And Peter said unto them, Repent ye, and be baptized every one of you in the name of Jesus Christ unto the remission of your sins; and ye shall receive the gift of the Holy Spirit (Acts 2:37-38).

Evangelization aimed at conversion has been the pattern established by Christ and carried forward by his Church since the beginning. Our day is no different. The weakness and imperfection of our current allies is also no different; we evangelize anyway.

THE ALLIES OF THE ENEMY

Thus far the enemy seems formidable. Not only is there a supernatural enemy to deal with but also an enemy that lurks within ourselves and in all possible human allies. It gets worse. The devil is our chief external enemy but by no means the only one; he has allies both witting and unwitting. These additional external enemies can be institutional, cultural, and human.

Institutional Enemies

The Church itself can be an unwitting accomplice to our enemy. Though Christ founded it and gave it the protection of the Holy Spirit, it can get in the way simply by its own bureaucratic and slow-moving nature. Some might balk at this and repeat the claim they have heard that Jesus did not come to found a Church. An honest reading of the New Testament, and particularly the Gospels, tells a different story. St. Matthew and the Holy Spirit tell us that Jesus identified St. Peter as the rock on which he would build his Church (Matt. 16:15-19). The same Gospel shows that the Church is to be the arbiter of justice on Earth, with the ability to cast people from its ranks (Matt. 18:15-18).

In Luke's Gospel, Christ says that those who reject the preaching of his chosen ones reject him and his Father. The Acts of the Apostles shows us both the first Church council and the first encyclical letter (Acts 15). Christ did found a Church, and it was a hierarchical organization with Peter at its head. Although it became more organized (and more Roman) over time, the seeds were there from the beginning. Not only did it become more organized, it became—for good and ill—more human.

The devil's trick is to undermine the authority of the Church. Not by attacking authority as such; even without his help, most Americans are disposed against outside authority. Rather, he seeks to undermine love. If he can convince people that the Church does not speak with the love of God, then he can wean them away from her using their own concupiscent and natural tendency to rebel against authority. So the Church responds with an increased emphasis on love. But when that love is presented or conceived as a love absent discipline, it plays into the diabolical plan. The Church is correct in emphasizing love; but it is mistaken to do so in a manner where love is not connected to discipline. What is needed is a demonstration of love that includes both discipline and authority.

Here the natural knowledge of parental love as necessarily including discipline and correction can be used as leverage. The Church teaches with a binding authority not simply because it has that authority (though it does—see Luke 10:16). The Church teaches because it loves. Denying someone the truth can never be a loving act, so the Church teaches what it learns from Christ. Its teaching needs to be presented as a love that is ordered toward getting souls to heaven. It is love that sees the dangerous path and warns—even forcibly—to not take the path, because it knows where that path leads. Just as God desires that all men be saved (see 1 Tim. 2:4), so too does the Church; even if it may seem harsh in the immediate event, it is far less harsh than an eternity irredeemably cut off from God's presence. Yes, love is the answer; but it must be a love capable of rebuke.

True love aims at the true good. When it stings, it is because the person being loved was pursuing a false good. The Church can be an obstacle, because it speaks hard truths that are hard to hear. But it does so with the authority of its founder.

This leads us into the consideration of the Church in its most unflattering light. This spotless bride of Christ has become mottled and bears the wounds it suffers from the spiritual combat. Here we must do as all good intelligence officers do and "think red": if Christ left behind a Church with an authority to teach in his name, and this truth will set one free, then attack the credibility of the Church as teacher. In this arena, the Church has played into the hands of the forces arrayed against it. Without trying to present a history lesson on the faults of the Church, I wish to bring up two instances in modern times where the credibility of the Church was attacked, and it allowed the attack to succeed or served as an unwitting accomplice.

The first of these two examples is the publication of, and the reaction to, the encyclical letter *Humanae Vitae*. In this document, Pope Paul VI applied the consistent and universal Church teaching about human sexuality to the situation brought about by the introduction of the birth control pill (a topic we will re-visit in the following section). The Catholic reaction to this document was widespread dissent; not only from the lay faithful but also from theologians and priests. In the face of this rebellion, the shepherds folded. With one exception, the bishops stood by and did nothing to rein in the voices urging the faithful to refuse obedience to what had been the teaching of the Church since the writing of the *Didache* in the late first or early second century. The courage of the bishops was tested and found wanting. As a result, people were emboldened to challenge other areas of Church teaching that challenged the modern age.

Our second example is the priestly sexual abuse crisis, first exposed in the U.S. but present in other (mostly Western) countries as well. When incidents were exposed to the bishops, far too many of them reacted as managers rather than shepherds, as bureaucrats rather than soldiers. It is true that in some cases "experts" in the fields of psychology and criminology told them that the desire to have sex with minors was curable. Once treated, often the offending priests were moved to new parishes, where many of them abused again. It took a long time to realize that this perversion cannot be cured by any means of which the counseling professions know.

Perhaps it was out of horror and repugnance that bishops kept things secret. Perhaps it was out of misplaced sympathy for men who suffered from same-sex attraction. In any case, the scourge of Sodom and Gomorrah showed its head, and too often the reaction was either fear or complicity. The authority given the bishops by Christ was wasted. Only time will tell if that trust can be rebuilt.

There are other institutional allies for our adversary, both intentional and unintentional. Staying with the Church and her unintentional aid to the adversary, one can cite the state of catechesis from the late 1970s onward. The old *Baltimore Catechism* and Sr. Mary Rapknuckles were replaced by education-as-entertainment. The incarnate second Person of the most holy Trinity became the happy hippie from Palestine who wanted to be everyone's friend. Fear of God (one of the gifts of the Holy Spirit) was replaced by "awe and reverence" before God. Perfect love does indeed cast out all fear, but there is nothing perfect on this side of heaven. What had been basic training for spiritual combat became spring break, and the troops became soft.

This was intentional in the sense that it was done as a means of making the Faith come alive for a new generation. What was unintentional was (at least) two generations of Catholics so poorly formed in the Faith that they could not withstand the pressures of the world. Christians had always been called to be in the world but not of the world. This new form of catechesis told them that the world was not a place of pilgrimage to be endured but a fun place where one could find contentment. This was occurring at the same time the culture was coarsening. Increased rates of crime, infidelity, divorce, and a general lowering of moral standards were taking place at the same time that basic training was becoming soft.

Cultural Enemies

So what was going on in the wider culture at the same time Catholics were experiencing catechism "lite"? The Age of Aquarius ushered in a real questioning of everything. In many areas, things that had once been unthinkable or unspeakable (at least in polite society) became commonplace and even celebrated. Three examples of the cultural shift can serve to illustrate the trend.

The first is the practice of abortion. California and New York were the first states to legalize abortion, albeit with certain limits. In less than a decade, laws were changed in all fifty states and the District of Columbia to allow abortion at any time before birth and without any meaningful restriction. Today, in the U.S. alone, around 3,000 abortions are performed daily.

The arguments in favor of legalized abortion were made in the name of compassion for the women experiencing unintended pregnancy. Of course, the numbers of women in that situation had been drastically increased by the aforementioned widespread use of oral contraceptives. Once people thought they had a reliable means to ensure pregnancy did not occur as a result of intercourse, the incidents of intercourse increased. And they increased precisely among those who had already made the decision not to bring a new life into the world. As a result, the need arose for a solution to the very problem that the Pill had been sold as a means of avoiding.

Thanks to two Supreme Court rulings, the killing of innocent human beings became accepted, then celebrated, and now vigorously defended. How did such a shift in public opinion occur in so short a time? Marketing and deception. Bernard Nathanson, a founder of the group now known as NARAL (National Abortion Rights Action League), has told the story often. The horror stories about coat hangers and back-alley abortions were simply fabricated to create the impression that there was a real crisis. After creating the crisis, the same forces offered a solution that relied on slick marketing to avoid the fact that termination of a human life was intended.

At the same time, "no-fault" divorce laws were introduced (again with California and New York in the lead). What had once been rare and understood as a tragedy for all involved became quick and simple. It too was sold in the name of compassion, and any idea that bad consequences would follow was swept under the rug. Today, we know that children of divorced parents are at vastly increased risk for any number of problems: poverty, crime, drug use, and their own likelihood as adults of divorce.

Divorce makes children worse off emotionally and economically, in addition to raising the odds that children from broken homes will break up their own homes as adults (and fall into crime, drugs, become a teen mom, get sick, pick up smoking, have a stroke . . . and die young). By making it easier to break up a home, no-fault divorce only makes it more likely that parents will commit this injustice against their children. Even one-time champions of no-fault divorce like feminist Betty Friedan now think it was a big mistake.

Our third example of a dramatic cultural shift is the reaction to people who suffer same-sex attraction or homosexuality. Like our other two examples, the speed of change in attitude from disapproval to celebration has been head-spinning. The sin that once was condemned by the vast majority of people in this country has become not just accepted but celebrated. Like the other examples, this change came about through a detailed and determined effort using psychological and marketing techniques while obscuring the true nature of the activity involved. In his book *The Marketing of Evil*, David Kupelian presents detailed evidence of exactly how these and other changes took place so completely in a relatively short time.

This, then, is the cultural milieu into which generations of poorly catechized Catholics are thrown. It is no wonder that they are unprepared to face the challenges presented to them. They are thrust into the thick of the spiritual combat utterly untrained and disarmed. The smoke of Satan certainly pollutes the larger culture. But to lay the blame on only him is simplistic and misleading.

Our fallen human nature shares the blame; so too does our intense desire to simply "get along" with others. All around us, the culture was changing rapidly and in directions Christianity had stood against since its inception. At the same time, Catholics were being urged to no longer see the world as a "veil of tears" or a place of pilgrimage. Rather they were to see it as the blossoming of the promised kingdom of God.

The Church was not at its best during the decades of the 1960s and '70s, but it was not simply an unwitting accomplice to the cultural degradation. There were attempts to fight against the tide, but they largely failed. Pope Paul VI sounded a warning that now appears to be prophetic. Speaking about artificial contraception, he warned:

Responsible men can become more deeply convinced of the truth of the doctrine laid down by the Church on this issue if they reflect on the consequences of methods and plans for artificial birth control. Let them first consider how easily this course of action could open wide the way for marital infidelity and a general lowering of moral standards. Not much experience is needed to be fully aware of human weakness and to understand that human beings—and especially the young, who are so exposed to temptation—need incentives to keep the moral law, and it is an evil thing to make it easy for them to break that law. Another effect that gives cause for alarm is that a man who grows accustomed to the use of contraceptive methods may forget the reverence due to a woman, and, disregarding her physical and emotional equilibrium, reduce her to being a mere instrument for the satisfaction of his own desires, no longer considering her as his partner whom he should surround with care and affection.

Finally, careful consideration should be given to the danger of this power passing into the hands of those public authorities who care little for the precepts of the moral law. Who will blame a government which in its attempt to resolve the problems affecting an entire country resorts to the same measures as are regarded as lawful by married people in the solution of a particular family difficulty? Who will prevent public authorities from favoring those contraceptive methods which they consider more effective? Should they regard this as necessary, they may even impose their use on everyone. It could well happen, therefore, that when people, either individually or in family or social life, experience the inherent difficulties of the divine law and are determined to avoid them, they may give into the hands of public authorities the power to intervene in the most personal and intimate responsibility of husband and wife (*Humanae Vitae* 17).

As already noted, this warning went unheeded, particularly by those charged with the duty to support it. One of the tasks of the New Evangelization is to recapture the received wisdom of Christianity and to present it as love by living joyfully according to it. Only by being a sign of loving contradiction to the ways of the world can the damage be healed.

Human Agency as a Purposeful Enemy

The ways in which human agency has contributed to the enemy in the spiritual combat are many. Often, they are done out of good motives. The quite foreseeable negative effects are ignored. In other cases, human actions gave rise to unforeseeable consequences. For example, public education abandoned training in formal logic so that people were more susceptible to the marketing campaigns that led to abrupt societal changes in attitudes. People lost the ability to recognize falsehood and to counter it with reasoned argument.

A similarly subtle unintended negative effect was the push to define religion as a private affair between the believer and his God. This was ostensibly done so that civil society might be more harmonious. People could live, work, and socialize in the great melting pot we call our home country, so long as religious differences were set aside.

It is a fact of history that one of the great gifts our country has provided to the rest of the world is a demonstration that a religiously diverse nation can still be a unified and strong nation. The wars following the Protestant Reformation in Europe convinced our Founding Fathers that there must be a better way. That better way was freedom of religion (in general) and lack of a state religion (in particular).

But as Seamus Hasson has shown in his book *The Right to Be Wrong*, this strength was problematic since the first colonists set foot on American soil. The history of our country shows both the perils and the strengths of this experiment in ordered liberty. One effect has been that, in order to foster civic unity, there has been an inexorable push to confine the free exercise of religion into a specific building, for a limited time on a particular day. Although one could be tempted to cite various legislative actions or court decisions as the root of this problem, it is simply a natural human tendency to get along with one another and to minimize areas of conflict.

Unfortunately, this has the effect of making religion a private affair between the individual and God. No longer does one understand that all of the Church is the mystical body of Christ and that religion is meant to inform all aspects of the life of the believer. Religion ceases to be something we are and becomes something we do.

At its worst, this attitude causes the believer to shrink from engaging in the public square with religiously based arguments meant to influence the larger society. I challenge the reader to read (or re-read) Martin Luther King Jr.'s "Letter from a Birmingham Jail" and ask himself how such an appeal would be received by the larger public today. To his credit, King used arguments from the Founding Fathers and the ancient Greeks to ensure his message was not based solely on Christianity. But, as befits a Baptist minister, the argument for justice was thoroughly Christian—Scripture, St. Augustine, and St. Thomas Aquinas are the central pillars of his writing. Would King today be accused of trying to shove his religion down the throat of the modern atheist? My bet is that the effect now would be markedly different than it was in 1963.

There are multiple forces at work, some even intended for good purposes. But the enemy is cunning, and he is able to use multiple strategies simultaneously and even enlist others in his cause without them becoming aware they are being used. He is a master at asymmetrical warfare.

The forces arrayed against faith are strong. They are led by a demon that is ever vigilant. He never sleeps and never rests. He has no real power where Christ is truly made present, but he never misses the chance to attack when the guard is not on watch. The Prince of Lies can wield power when opportunity is left open to him. The best historical analog I can think of to capture this situation came in the waning days of the battle for Peleliu during World War II. The Japanese had convinced many of the inhabitants that, if they fell into the hands of the U.S. forces, they would be subject to rape, torture, and murder. U.S. forces watched in horror as hundreds of women and children jumped (or were thrown) to their deaths from what became known as the "suicide cliffs." Loudspeakers were set up across the ravine so that interpreters could try to stop the madness. But the lie had taken hold, and souls were lost.

This is the state of the battlefield. The enemy has sown his lies deep and wide, and many innocent people are under his sway. The New Evangelization is not just about putting fannies back in the pews (and money back in the collection plate): it is a spiritual combat to win back souls. The enemy's most likely course of action is to attack any opening he can find or make, using any ally he can find, coerce, or deceive. His most dangerous course of action is to attack the credibility of the Church founded by Christ. He cannot defeat Christ; but he is hard at work on the Church. The call to arms is sounded.

TERRAIN AND OBSTACLE ANALYSIS: BARRIERS TO CONVERSION

Part of the intelligence section of an operations order is an analysis of the terrain (the ground over which one intends to move and fight) and any obstacles—natural or man-made—

that might be encountered. The aim is to understand how the terrain itself can aid or hinder one's plans. This analysis can go a long way to shaping how one approaches the fight.

Terrain

Part of the plan is to understand what ground to avoid and what ground to employ. Our case is no different. As a first step, we outline certain areas as "no-go" terrain. In a military operation, this might be a swamp or a dense forest impassable for vehicles. The terrain can be a danger all by itself. For our purposes, we will consider where *not* to evangelize: funerals and weddings, for instance, even though one may be strongly inclined to do so because they are the two occasions we most often see those who are dear to us who have fallen away from the Faith. These occasions, though normally religious in nature, are not good ground for us. Attempts to evangelize here will likely be met with deserved hostility, because they detract from the purpose of the gathering.

Other "no-go" terrain includes the workplace—especially if you are the boss. Social gatherings are also, if not "no-go" areas, at least dangerous ground. Attempts to evangelize in these situations lead to charges that one is trying to shove one's religion down the throats of others. This is because overt evangelization here is simply out of place. The old line about dinner parties has some truth: leave politics and religion out of it.

This may seem to be at odds with what has been presented thus far. The reader may be wondering what situations in life are *not* "no-go" areas. Is the battlespace shrinking to almost nothing? It depends on the tactics used. Certainly defensive measures are allowed on any ground. If one is questioned or confronted, it is always proper to give a defense of one's faith (see 1 Pet. 3:15). Do not hide from confrontation or hide your faith, but respond to hostility with both charity and clarity (charity first).

Overt attempts at evangelization, unless invited, do more harm than good. Rather, conduct yourself in such a manner as others will want to know what makes you tick. This will eventually lead to questions that are not hostile, even though the questions may come much later. It is not uncommon that one's actions in the past (even a distant past) will lead to questions in the future. But these openings are precious, because they are an indication that the questioner has been prepared by the Holy Spirit (even if he understands it only as curiosity). There is a desire to know—and that is a better place to plant a seed than on rocky ground.

Obstacles

The next step in the planning process is to identify some of the major barriers to conversion. This is a complex task; some of these barriers apply only to certain segments of the population. In other cases, certain people may be restrained by more than one of these barriers. At this point, the task is to simply identify them. In the next chapter we will address ways in which these obstacles may be overcome.

It is important to note that, in any good obstacle plan, each obstacle should be covered by fire and the obstacles should be placed so that they are mutually supporting (each one makes the others more effective). In our analysis of the battlespace, we can see that they are indeed mutually supporting. They are linked by common elements so that a person encountering one obstacle will naturally encounter others as well. They are also covered by fire. In martial terms, this means that the obstacle has some form of direct or indirect fire weapon that can engage any forces attempting to reduce or bypass it. It follows then that the obstacle must also be under observation so that the weapons can be fired as needed. In spiritual combat, we find that the weapons used to cover the obstacle with fire are largely cultural but at times may be governmental. We will address these portions of the plan after our description of the obstacles themselves.

Obstacles in Training

I wish to begin with the obstacles that face those who are already practicing the Faith to some degree. I begin here because these are our allies. If one can set them free from their barriers, they can join us in the fight. We will need their help in the battle against those who are indifferent. We need all our allies and weapons in the fight against those who are actively hostile to faith. The first difficulty believers face is not realizing the need for conversion. Such people might feel that they have no need for conversion. They have been baptized and confirmed, they attend Mass. But they do not see themselves as called to take part in the spiritual combat and the New Evangelization. They are our allies but have chosen the rear area over the front lines.

Many people see conversion as a singular event; either being baptized or "accepting Jesus Christ as one's personal Lord and Savior." There is no doubt that these events are significant. Baptism, of course, removes original sin and makes one a member of the Mystical Body of Christ. One becomes a child of God and a co-heir to heaven. St. Paul writes about this in his letter to the Church at Rome:

> For all who are led by the Spirit of God are sons of God. For you did not receive the spirit of slavery to fall back into

fear, but you have received the spirit of sonship. When we cry, "Abba! Father!" it is the Spirit himself bearing witness with our spirit that we are children of God, and if children, then heirs, heirs of God and fellow heirs with Christ, provided we suffer with him in order that we may also be glorified with him. I consider that the sufferings of this present time are not worth comparing with the glory that is to be revealed to us (Rom. 8:14-17).

Since most Christians are baptized as infants (or at least while young), there is a need for baptized persons to grasp the Faith on their own and for themselves. One may hope that this would occur with the sacraments of Confirmation and Eucharist, but they might not be complete. From an ecclesial perspective, these two sacraments complete initiation. But there is an interior event that one hopes would precede them but may actually follow. That interior attitude of deciding to live by the Spirit and not by the flesh is often summed up by the phrase popular among our Evangelical brethren where one "accepts Jesus Christ as one's personal Lord and Savior." These events are significant, but they are not sufficient.

To see them as any more than an initiation into Christ is to misunderstand the nature of conversion. Conversion is not a one-time event but a lifelong process. Fr. Garrigou-Lagrange bases this fact on the lives of the apostles. They were initially converted when Christ called them to leave their fishing boats, or tax booth, and follow him. Over the three years of his public ministry, they came to know him and his message until St. Peter could say, "You are the Christ, the Son of the living God" (Matt. 16:16).

But even after this new depth of conversion, they all abandoned him; St. Peter even denied knowing him. It was not until they received the Holy Spirit at Pentecost that they were ready to begin the work they had been called to do. If even the apostles were in need of a series of conversions, it would be a safe bet we all are in similar need. Conversion is a process of an ever-deeper encounter with Christ. There is always more that can be done until the day we see him face to face in heaven—that is when conversion is complete (and never before then).

Minor Obstacles

Our potential allies may be avoiding the front lines of battle because they do not know the nature of the fight. But there are other reasons for timidity. The novelist Flannery O'Conner summed up the situation when she wrote, "You will know the truth, and the truth will make you odd." Many Christians avoid evangelization because it is uncomfortable. If they speak too openly of their faith with anyone but their own closest Christian friends, they will suffer. In this country they will not suffer as St. Peter and St. Paul did—at least in the U.S. for the time being.

What today's evangelical Catholic must suffer ranges between ostracization from polite society and full-fledged hostility. The more benign end of that spectrum begins with being labeled as "closed-minded" or (gasp) "judgmental." Although these are mild wounds to suffer, they are the most common and therefore the ones that must be addressed first. They will be addressed at length for two reasons: because they are so common and because they are often the barriers people cannot move beyond.

What is "closed-mindedness"? It can be defined as the unwillingness to allow new or alternative points of view to enter into one's conscious deliberation about a given topic. Fair enough. The more difficult question is to properly *identify* instances of closed-mindedness. For what may appear as such may also be evidence of the exact opposite. In the vast majority of cases where this accusation is made, the accuser has no idea what led a person to hold a certain view. The charge of being closed-minded is really just a way of saying, "I disagree and find your position offensive." This charge is often made because it is effective as a conversation ender. When accused of closed-mindedness, most people retreat from further discussion. In our obstacle-breaching plan, we will see that there is a way to defeat this common but formidable obstacle.

A related obstacle is being called "judgmental." The one scriptural admonition that every atheist seems to know is "Judge not"! Of course, they are mistaken about exactly what that admonition means; and most Christians are as well. Christ tells his disciples not to pass judgment on others. At the same time, he tells us quite clearly to make judgments about the actions people take and to treat them accordingly (Matt. 18:15-18, 1 Cor. 5).

Even if being judgmental does not mean what many people think it means, it is still uncomfortable when one is accused of being so. Like closed-mindedness, it is a conversation stopper, because most people do not know how to respond. In reality, being judgmental is not only a Christian virtue, it is part of the foundation of civilized society. Why this is the case and how one responds to the charge are also covered in the obstacle-breaching plan.

The New Testament is full of warnings about passing judgments on others. It is also full of commands to judge the actions of others and to treat them in accordance with those actions. Since the former are so well known, let us examine a few of the latter.

In one of his letters to the Church at Corinth, St. Paul writes that he has heard there is a man among them who is living in an incestuous relationship with his own mother (or stepmother). St. Paul's reaction is strong:

> It is actually reported that there is immorality among you, and of a kind that is not found even among pagans; for a man is living with his father's wife. And you are arrogant! Ought you not rather to mourn? Let him who has done this be removed from among you. For though absent in body I am present in spirit, and as if present, I have already pronounced judgment in the name of the Lord Jesus on the man who has done such a thing. When you are assembled, and my spirit is present, with the power of our Lord Jesus, you are to deliver this man to Satan for the destruction of the flesh, that his spirit may be saved in the day of the Lord Jesus (1 Cor. 5:1-5).

Now, some might contend that this was an extreme example—and it was. So turn to Jesus' words in Matthew's Gospel:

> If your brother sins against you, go and tell him his fault, between you and him alone. If he listens to you, you have gained your brother. But if he does not listen, take one or two others along with you, that every word may be confirmed by the evidence of two or three witnesses. If he refuses to listen to them, tell it to the church; and if he refuses to listen even to the church, let him be to you as a Gentile and a tax collector" (Matt. 18:15-17).

Here the sin is not specified, but the penalty is the same: the one who refuses to repent is cast out of the Church. In fact, the New Testament is full of exhortations to warn and admonish sinners; and to reject those who persist in their sins. This is why the spiritual works of mercy include such things as Instructing the ignorant and rebuking the sinner (see CCC 2447). This is done not because we are better than them but for their own repentance and conversion. To warn others they are sinners is an act of love. It is an attempt to help them avoid the fate of those who remain in their sins:

> Do you not know that the unrighteous will not inherit the kingdom of God? Do not be deceived; neither the immoral, nor idolaters, nor adulterers, nor sexual perverts, nor thieves, nor the greedy, nor drunkards, nor revilers, nor robbers will inherit the kingdom of God (1 Cor. 6:9-10).

So how can the word of God, inspired by the Holy Spirit, be contradictory? Does the Holy Spirit "speak against" himself? Of course not. "All scripture is inspired by God and profitable for teaching, for reproof, for correction, and for training in righteousness" (2 Tim. 3:16). Since it is inspired by God, who is love (see 1 John 4:8), then love and judgment must be compatible. God cannot be divided against himself, nor can his revelation in Scripture. Hans Urs von Balthasar addresses this problem when he writes:

> If we fail to let the word's sharp edge have its effect on us, we shall always be meeting the merely imaginary Redeemer; if we fail to face the judgment of Christ every time we contemplate, we shall not perceive the distinctive quality of divine grace. The consuming fire of crucified Love is both redemption and judgment; the two are inseparable and indistinguishable.[7]

---

7. Hans Urs von Balthasar, *Prayer* (San Francisco: Ignatius Press, 1986), 224–5.

When faced by such a paradox, one simply looks for a deeper understanding that would reconcile both the command not to judge and the assurance that one must judge. The key is found in one of the titles given to Jesus in Scripture. He, and he alone, is the "Just Judge." What is the nature of his judgment? It is to determine the fate of one's eternal soul. This form of judgment is one that the individual Christian may not dare to make. Judgments about what actions are sinful—and the treatment of the unrepentant—are absolutely necessary. How do we know this? Again, we turn to that problematic group of Christians at Corinth:

> When one of you has a grievance against a brother, does he dare go to law before the unrighteous instead of the saints? Do you not know that the saints will judge the world? And if the world is to be judged by you, are you incompetent to try trivial cases? Do you not know that we are to judge angels? How much more, matters pertaining to this life! (1 Cor. 6:1-3).

So these two most common obstacles are also the easiest to overcome. Not that the ostracizing will cease, but the Christian need have no fear of it.

The Major Obstacle (in Various Forms)

What then of the other, more serious end of the spectrum for the believer? What of the open hostility one will likely face after explaining why one is neither closed-minded nor judgmental?

Many of the more serious obstacles are experienced in different ways by different people. Some are faced with a multitude of obstacles and others with perhaps one or two large ones. Even the person experiencing the obstacle may not be able to clearly perceive what the difficulty actually is. Our task here is to describe, in generic terms, what the obstacles are. In Chapter 3 we will offer some insights on how these obstacles are to be addressed. Exactly how they can be reduced or bypassed will be dependent on the experiences of the person encountering them.

The major obstacle is the idea that God is not real and that religion is either delusional (at best) or a nefarious means of controlling others. These views have existed alongside religions and ideas about God for most of recorded history. Today they seem to be gaining strength. Atheists and agnostics have always existed, but they have also always been a distinct minority. Today, particularly in the affluent West, their numbers are larger than ever. But, as we noted earlier, the U.S. is unique in that the vast majority of the population remains committed—to a degree—to the idea of God and the practice of religion. While most people still self-identify as a member of a religion, the strength of that commitment is often questionable.

This, of course, goes to the previously identified center of gravity. God may be real, but once he begins to make demands, adherence to his commandments weakens. This is the primary obstacle, because it is the basis of so many of the others. While most people in this country would not consider themselves atheists or agnostics, many are approaching that status functionally.

But what of the self-identified atheist or agnostic? We begin with the latter mindset, since it is most easily addressed. The agnostic is one who has no opinion on the question of God (or gods). For this person, the question is of no interest and no importance. To a degree, he looks at the believer and the atheist and says, "A pox on both your houses." These folks are rare; scratch most self-identified agnostics and you find an atheist who is unsure of his convictions—and lousy at formal logic.

The atheist is convinced that the question of God (or gods) is terribly important and that it must be answered in the negative. For him, religion and the idea of God is something that most people have not sufficiently thought through, and he considers it his duty to help his fellow man see through this problem. As I mentioned earlier, I have no intention of addressing particular arguments of the "New Atheists," because that is falling prey to the very obstacle they have erected. Here we provide a sketch of some of the main lines of thought.

An atheist's theories tend to reflect his background. For some, the idea of God is a byproduct of evolution, the need for which humanity has outgrown. In this view, the social cohesion and obedience fostered by religion gave its adherents an edge in the battle for survival and evolutionary success. Since we no longer live in an era where social cohesion is necessary for survival; religion no longer offers an evolutionary advantage and ought to disappear.

A related theory is that there is a God-gene. This too existed for the benefit of survival and was passed along as a dominant gene form. Presumably, the disappearance (or suppression) of the gene will take place, as it is no longer necessary. How long the gene will continue its effect, or if it is cultural rather than genetic, is difficult to say.

Yet others see religion not as a product of evolution, but of ignorance. Certainly there were times when unexplained phenomena were chalked up to God/the gods. As knowledge, and particular knowledge of the physical sciences, progressed, man had less need to explain things as an "act of God." Once the state of man's knowledge (in general) has made sufficient progress, the tendency to believe in God/gods will cease.

For the atheists who hold this view, our current knowledge of the world not only precludes the need to point to God/gods as explanatory; science itself has shown that God does not exist. These atheists have advanced sufficiently in knowledge, and the rest of us just need to catch up. This claim has been made with regularity since (at least) the Age of the Enlightenment.

These are a few of the prominent ideas offered by atheists. Closely aligned with these views is the notion that the only things we can know to be true come from mathematics and/or the empirical sciences. This notion betrays a lack of knowledge about the history of science itself. Many of the things science has "proven" to be true have been upended because a scientist questioned the "scientific truth" and replaced it with a better one. Lack of historical knowledge is only one reason for the idea that truth can come only from empirical science.

Another reason is the desire to avoid controversy. No one seriously doubts that $2 + 2 = 4$, or that the laws of physics exist; at least most people do not argue about these things. But there is almost no end of controversy surrounding the truth claims proposed by religion (and philosophy), particularly in the realm of morality. A simple way to avoid taking a side in the controversy is to claim that the truth in such areas is simply not knowable until it can be proven by science (math does not help too often on moral matters).

Related to the questions about non-scientific truth is the idea that "truth" itself is not knowable. This can take the more common form of subjectivism, where each person is free to decide what is true or not true for him. It can also take the form of nihilism, which sees the word *truth* as having no real meaning. Normally the difference between those holding either view is a function of how much philosophy the person has read. For those with no philosophical background, the temptation is to subjectivism. Having not thought deeply about the existence of objective truth, or the human necessity to seek it, being able to decide one's own truth is quite appealing. Those who have thought deeply about such matters and read at least some philosophy can be tempted to think that the there is no truth, since many contradictory arguments seem to be well made. One therefore concludes that all "truth" is merely construct, and even our ability to communicate is but an illusion, since we have no fixed meaning for anything.

Supporting Obstacles

Supporting obstacles are dependent on the larger ones for their effectiveness. We have already addressed the agnostic, for whom the questions about God/gods or "truth" simply do not matter. We have also described various approaches to truth. The offshoots of these ideas are obstacles such as seeing questions about God/god and objective truth as too difficult or time-consuming to solve. One is better off simply leaving aside such great questions and focusing on the day's activities and tasks. There may in fact be an answer to those questions, but there are simply not enough hours in the day to waste time on finding them. Even if there were time, would the answers make any difference? There are still chores to be done, and the football game begins in an hour.

The next obstacle to be considered is the loss of the concept of sin. In a 1950s-era Christmas radio address, Archbishop Giovanni Battista Montini—who became Pope Paul VI—said that the primary sin of the twentieth century was a loss of the sense of sin. Already in his day the word *sin* was either being neglected or replaced with words like *weakness* or *error*. Sin is, of course, a sign of our finite weaknesses, and it can even be an error (though not a mistake). A consequence of shying away from the powerful word *sin* has been to detach the activity from the sanction. Montini's lament was that the effect was so widespread that the idea of what sin is (an offense against God and oneself) and its effect (estrangement or separation from God) were forgotten. This only became more widespread as psychology and psychological categories came to dominate the public understanding of human actions. Once our culture had reached the Lake Wobegon (or Barney the Dinosaur) stage, the absence of sin was the norm. We are no longer all sinners, but we *are* all special.

Our final obstacle is the area of human sexuality. Often those who are opposed to what the Church teaches about human sexuality claim that it is too focused on "pelvic issues." They note that the current pope has called for less attention to these topics. What they fail to mention is that Pope Benedict XVI said much the same thing. The difference is that Benedict pointed out that the reason why the Church seems focused on sex is that it is the area most often challenged by detractors. In reality, the Church is not obsessed with sex; its opponents are.

This is not limited to Catholicism by any means. The recent breakup within the ELCA (Evangelical Lutheran Church of America) and the pending one in the Anglican Church are over sexual matters. Ecclesial communion has been broken, or is on the verge of breaking, over the ordination of active homosexuals. The struggle over the proper role and definitions of healthy and moral human sexuality is not even limited to the Church versus the popular culture. These questions arise in politics, science, and business as well.

It seems that there is confusion and anxiety about sex almost anywhere you look. It also seems that sex is almost anywhere you look. Popular media, advertising, and music seem to be guilty of the same focus on "pelvic issues." It is beyond the scope of this operations order to solve such broad cultural problems (at least directly). Our task (in general) is to address questions of human sexuality from a religious perspective. The task for the obstacle analysis is to describe it. In the breeching plan, we will present the course of action to reduce it.

The way in which human sexuality acts as an obstacle is that the Church *seems* to say "no" and "stop," while the larger culture says "yes" and "more." Many people are afraid of commitment and conversion, because they think if they follow the path of faith, they will be missing out on one of the greatest pleasures one can have in this life. For some, this comes across as an unjust and unlivable imposition on human freedom and happiness.

This very real obstacle is built largely on two things: ignorance and marketing. These two factors are mutually supporting; each one aids and increases the other. The ignorance is about what the Church actually has to say about human sexuality. My experience has shown me that "everyone knows" what the Church teaches about sex; but no one has actually read what the Church has to say.

The popular culture assumes that Christians believe sex is bad and dirty; we wish God had not made it the means of continuing the species. We are even more offended that he made it pleasurable. Most troubling is that, somewhere, someone might be having a good time—and this we cannot tolerate.

The marketing aspect is not just the pervasiveness of sex: those girls in bikinis do not really drink that much beer. (If they did, their figures would look very different.) The chief message being marketed is this: Everyone is "doing it" (and "it" can mean many different things), and if you aren't, then you are not only missing out, you are being oppressed.

Because sex is such a powerful human motivation, it does not take much effort to turn it into an obstacle. Given the factors of ignorance and marketing, it is one that will take a determined effort to overcome. The obstacle breeching plan will provide the basics.

2

MISSION

THE MISSION PARAGRAPH IS A CONCISE, DIRECT STATEMENT OF THE TASKS TO BE ACHIEVED: WHAT, WHERE, WHEN, AND WHY. IF AND WHEN THE PLAN BEGINS TO BREAK DOWN, THE ONE THING THAT MUST REMAIN CLEAR IS THE MISSION.

In contrast to the other portions of an operations order, the mission portion is quite short—usually no longer than three sentences. This allows for clarity: in the event that effective control of subordinate units is lost or compromised, those units can still function if they know the *mission*.

In a small-unit operations order, battalion level[8] or smaller, the mission statement is the one part of a five-paragraph order that resembles an actual paragraph. There is one form of operation order, however, that is different in this regard, and that is the "mission-type" order. Normally used for asymmetrical combat, the mission-type order focuses on describing the mission rather than the execution. This is done because, in asymmetrical combat, the unit leader is not sure where the enemy forces are, how they are arranged, or how they will react.

The fight against irregular guerrilla or terrorist forces is an example of this type of warfare. The man selling bread in the town square by day may be planting roadside bombs at night. The village elders one has tea with may be the fathers and

---

8. A battalion is normally 800 to 1,000 men at full strength, depending on the type of battalion (infantry, artillery, etc.).

uncles of the insurgents. In an asymmetrical fight, members of the enemy force understand that they cannot win in conventional warfare, so they use every means they can to disguise their intentions and tactics. Since this is the nature of the spiritual combat before us, this chapter will be a mission-type order. As always, there will be related materials presented here as well. But first: a clear description of the basic mission.

WHAT MISSION ENTAILS

The mission of this book is to present, in a simple yet thorough manner, the argument for and appeal of Christian truth for the purpose of contributing to the New Evangelization. The mission of both this spiritual combat and the New Evangelization is to get souls to heaven.

I have used the phrases *spiritual combat* and *New Evangelization* frequently and will continue to do so. It may seem that they are interchangeable, but this is not quite the case. They are intimately related, but there are important distinctions to be made on different levels. In the simplest analysis, *spiritual combat* is an inclusive term to designate an overall approach to the spiritual life. It seeks to introduce an offensive mindset and action-oriented approach to achieving holiness. This is the central goal of the book mentioned in the introduction, Dom Lorenzo's classic, *The Spiritual Combat*.

Interior Conversion First

In this book, the establishment of the offensive mindset is also a key intention. Christians are engaged in a battle for souls, even if they don't know it. Recall St. Peter's warning: "Be sober, be watchful: your adversary the devil prowls around like a roaring lion, seeking someone to devour" (1 Pet. 5:8).

One aspect of the spiritual combat is the New Evangelization. So spiritual combat is a larger term that includes, as one of its aspects, the New Evangelization. A second key distinction is that one must first engage in spiritual combat on a personal or interior level before one can engage in the New Evangelization. The inner battle must be fought before the larger battle can be joined. The overall goal is a personal holiness that can get souls to heaven after the pilgrim journey on Earth. One cannot lead others where one has not gone. One cannot give or foster what one does not have. From this perspective, we have a two-phased operation:

- Phase I: Interior spiritual combat to experience and deepen one's own conversion.

- Phase II: Exterior fruit of personal conversion is the New Evangelization—seeking to share the great joy one has found out of love for one's fellow man.

This is an important way of seeing both spiritual combat and New Evangelization. But, as is often the case in matters theological, it is incomplete and even misleading when left so simple. Although it is true that one must deepen one's own conversion before being a credible witness to others, it is not really a phase one/phase two approach. Phase one continues throughout phase two. If one were to cease phase one (deepening of personal conversion) in order to focus on phase two, it would be a sign he had not understood phase one. Conversion is a process, not an event. Engaging in the New Evangelization will challenge a Christian, and he will be in continual need of an ever-deeper conversion for himself. There are distinct phases, but they overlap.

Under Increasing Attack

Those who strive for personal holiness draw the immediate attention of the adversary. Once we engage in the fight, we come under increasing attack. It may be in the form of temptations never before experienced, or alienation (or distancing) from friends and loved ones. The attacks can take an almost limitless number of forms, but they must all be understood as attacks. The enemy will seek to counter any move one makes toward conversion of himself or others. Consider the words of St. Francis de Sales:

> Directly that your worldly friends perceive that you aim at leading a devout life, they will let loose endless shafts of mockery and misrepresentation upon you; the more malicious will attribute your change to hypocrisy, designing, or bigotry; they will affirm that the world having looked coldly upon you, failing its favor you turn to God; while your friends will make a series of what, from their point of view, are prudent and charitable remonstrances. They will tell you that you are growing morbid; that you will lose your worldly credit and will make yourself unacceptable to the world; they will prognosticate your premature old age, the ruin of your material prosperity; they will tell you that in the world you must live as the world does; that you can be saved without all this fuss; and much more of the like nature.[9]

Scupoli puts it this way:

> Such disciplined conduct is well fortified against the assaults of the devil. When this skilled opponent sees the fer-

9. St. Francis de Sales, *Introduction to the Devout Life*, part IV, ch. 1.

vor of persons beginning the spiritual exercises and the
fixed resolution of their wills, he insinuates his subtleties
into their understanding. A breakthrough here permits him
to push his way to the will. He is then the master of both
these faculties.[10]

The enemy and his allies will always react to people striving for holiness. The one engaging in the spiritual combat
must be prepared to suffer these and other assaults. To defend
against them, he must have constant recourse to prayer, the
sacraments, and spiritual practices. The enemy never rests, and
the process of conversion must never stop.

The warrior for God now has a clear mission: getting his
own soul and the souls of others to heaven. He understands
the two poles on which this mission revolves: personal conversion and, as a fruit of that conversion, the sharing of the
good news of salvation. He further understands how both
phases of the combat must be conducted: at first sequentially
and then simultaneously.

Our Mission: The Father's Will

In the Gospels, Christ makes it clear that he has come to accomplish the mission assigned to him by the Father. The Son
comes to Earth to do the Father's will (John 5:19) to the point
that it is the very source of his life (John 4:34), because he
and the Father are one (John 10:30). This is a unity of mission
and purpose that, while divine in nature, ought to serve as the
exemplar for all other missions.

Of course, this raises a question: what exactly is the Father's

---

10. Dom Lorenzo Scupoli, *The Spiritual Combat* (Rockford, IL: TAN Books and
Publishers, 1945), 24.

will? To further our analogy, what are the details about the mission? Again, the answer is simple and straightforward: to bring about the kingdom of God (Luke 4:43) by healing and preaching the good news of salvation:

> "The Spirit of the Lord is upon me, because he has anointed me to preach good news to the poor. He has sent me to proclaim release to the captives and recovering of sight to the blind, to set at liberty those who are oppressed, to proclaim the acceptable year of the Lord." And he closed the book, and gave it back to the attendant, and sat down; and the eyes of all in the synagogue were fixed on him. And he began to say to them, "Today this scripture has been fulfilled in your hearing" (Luke 4:18-21).

The mission he gives to his Church is similarly precise:

> "Go therefore and make disciples of all nations, baptizing them in the name of the Father and of the Son and of the Holy Spirit, teaching them to observe all that I have commanded you; and lo, I am with you always, to the close of the age" (Matt. 28:19-20).

Parish Mission

At one time in the not-too-distant past, many parishes spent considerable time and effort to develop their own mission statements, a practice adopted from the business world. It can have a salutary effect if it helps the parish members clarify who they are and what they are about. Too often, though, such a mission statement ends up being an exercise in self-aggrandizement and is simply a long list of all the wonderful things *we* are doing.

But to the extent that it departs from the mission already supplied by Christ, it is flawed. We have been given a mission statement; we do not need to make up our own. Most importantly, it is not about what we do but what *he* does. Parishes ought to keep in mind that they don't determine a mission for themselves; it comes from their higher headquarters.

Finally, the mission Christ gave the evangelists is clear:

And he said to them, "The harvest is plentiful, but the laborers are few; pray therefore the Lord of the harvest to send out laborers into his harvest. Go your way; behold, I send you out as lambs in the midst of wolves. Carry no purse, no bag, no sandals; and salute no one on the road. Whatever house you enter, first say, 'Peace be to this house!' And if a son of peace is there, your peace shall rest upon him; but if not, it shall return to you. [. . .] But whenever you enter a town and they do not receive you, go into its streets and say, 'Even the dust of your town that clings to our feet, we wipe off against you; nevertheless know this, that the kingdom of God has come near.' [. . .] He who hears you hears me, and he who rejects you rejects me, and he who rejects me rejects him who sent me" (Luke 10:2-16).

First, parish members must pray, because they are engaged in dangerous work (vv. 2-3). They are to bless (v. 5), to heal, and to preach the good news of salvation (v. 9). They must remain focused on the task at hand (v. 7). If they are rejected (for surely they will be), they must pass judgment on those who reject them (v. 11), because they act as a continuation of Christ's own mission (v. 16).

It is not their task to ensure their own success—that is left to the Holy Spirit acting in those who hear them. It is still as it was at Pentecost, when some in the crowd were moved to repentance and others to scoffing (Acts 2:6-13).

THE NATURE OF MISSION

To help us understand the simple mission—to get our own souls and those of others we encounter to heaven—we need to "unpack" the nature of the mission. The thoughts of the late, great Cardinal Hans Urs von Balthasar will be our guide. As we have already seen, Christ's mission was given him by the Father. Christ then gives this same mission to his followers (the disciples and apostles) and, by extension, to each baptized person. Just as in the military, there is a flow of mission from higher headquarters to subordinate units. At each step along the way the unit commander restates the mission he received in a manner fitting his own subordinates.

The same is true for spiritual combat. The mission has been given: from the Father to Christ and from Christ to us, mediated by the Holy Spirit.

Christian conversion brought about by a call from Jesus is not a monologue conducted by the lower and higher self of a person, but a dialogue between the sinner and his Lord who calls him to an accounting.[11]

Christ is the Father's Word to humanity. The Father speaks in his Son, and no one can come to the Father unless he comes through the Son. The dialogue between the human person and God is always centered in Christ. But because no member of the Trinity operates alone, dialogue is always Trinitarian, and the dialogue of conversion is no different. This is seen most clearly in the speech of St. Peter at Pentecost. Filled with the Holy Spirit, St. Peter spoke about Christ's saving works. In-

11. Balthasar, "Conversion in the New Testament," *Communio* (1, no. 1, 1974), 55–56.

spired by the same Holy Spirit, many in the crowd responded
with the question: "What must we do?" The answer was "Repent and believe in the Gospel." Simple, but also complex.

What happens to the person who is open to the work of the
Holy Spirit and begins to accept his mission and enter the
spiritual combat? (Later I will address those who reject the
call—or fail to fully embrace it). For Cardinal Balthasar,
the person becomes a "theological person." This means that
the person's life is changed and centered on the mission. This
is why God changed people's names in Scripture. Abram becomes Abraham, Jacob becomes Israel, Simon becomes Peter.

Personal Conversion

For the ancient Hebrews, a person's name signified who they
were and where they came from. So the significance of the
name change was to indicate that the person had become a
new person because of the mission he had been given. To
become a "theological person" was to allow the mission to
be at the center of one's life and to live as a new person. It is
worth noting that the Blessed Virgin did not receive a new
name. Because she was without sin, she required no transformation. She certainly did learn and experience the deeper
consequences of her mission, but she had already embraced
it fully. She needed only to continue to follow it and allow it
to work in her.

So personal conversion is accomplished by human cooperation with the Holy Spirit, and the first step is turning from sin
and becoming a new creation. This is accomplished primarily
through prayer. It is in contemplative prayer that the call to
decision is heard. It is also in prayer that the moment of decision is carried out. More properly, the moments of decision
are carried out because, while there is a single, unique mo-

ment where one responds with a foundational "yes," conversion is a continual conversation. God continually sets before the person the consequences of the initial "yes" and asks that a continual answer be given. The call is given continuously and individually; it must be heard and obeyed continuously.[12] At any point the call can become too much of a challenge and the human "yes" can become "Yes, but" or "Only if."

The call and response pattern is reflected in the Lord's conversation with Peter on the shore of the Sea of Tiberius (see John 21:15ff). Christ continually asks him, "Peter, do you love me?" Each affirmative answer leads to a command, "Feed my sheep." Finally, the conversation turns, and Christ tells Peter:

> Amen, amen, I say to you, when you were younger, you used to dress yourself and go where you wanted; but when you grow old, you will stretch out your hands, and someone else will dress you and lead you where you do not want to go" (John. 21:18).

As John tells us, the dialogue occurred so that Peter would come to realize that his continual "Yes" to Christ would result in his own death. This insight is not at all evident in the words spoken by Christ at that moment. It is only in hindsight that Peter would have been able to see the significance of those words as pointing to his own death. Prayer and reflection reveal the meaning, aided by the clarity Peter gained from the experience of imprisonment and the rejection that followed it. Christ's earthly mission took on final form only in the light of his own post-Resurrection teaching. The action of the Holy Spirit, along with prayer and contemplation, are always necessary to fully grasp the good news.

12. Balthasar, *The Christian State of Life* (San Francisco: Ignatius Press, 1983), 391.

Christ's Presence in the World

So conversion is dependent on prayer and unique to each individual. But it is not individualistic. The mission given by Christ can be accomplished only in the Church and never apart from her. On the one hand this is obvious; the Church on Earth is made up of people, and it can accomplish its mission only as a result of the conversion of its members. In Balthasar's view, the Church is always animated and guided by the Spirit, but the Church is *Christ's* presence in the world.

As Balthasar saw it, the effect of Christ is like an official's seal that was pressed into hot wax to authenticate a document. In this analogy, Jesus is the seal, and the hot wax is the history of the world, the Church, and each individual soul. All have been left with his imprint. The Holy Spirit impresses the form of Christ on mankind, and the Church is this imprint in history.[13] The Church is animated by the Holy Spirit; it presents and brings forth Christ, and, in spite of (or alongside) all this, it retains a human dimension that is crucial to the accomplishment of its mission.

The Church is often seen as either unnecessary for the Christian in his relationship with Christ or even as an obstacle. Balthasar understood why people are often disappointed that "the Kingdom was preached and we got the Church instead." Although he can understand the feeling, he will not abide in it. Without failing to acknowledge the "failures of love" in the history of the Church, he is always mindful of her divine aspects. He laments that the failures of love can so mask the divine nature of the Church that

13. Ibid., 562.

these hesitations make themselves felt right up to the moment of a final Christian decision: and so one reaches the threshold, about to decide for Christ, and one hears, "Jesus, yes; the Church, no!"[14]

We saw how true this is today when we considered the Church as an obstacle or even an unwitting ally of the enemy. The Church on Earth has failings because it is made up of sinners. It is simplistic to say that the failings of the Church are due to the frailties of her human members alone. The Church on Earth is also caught up in the battle depicted in the book of Revelation. Although particular failures may be attributed to her members, one cannot neglect the fact that supernatural forces are at work for both good and evil.

But now, for the rest of the story: Despite its failings, the Church perseveres, and, along with its wrinkles and spots (Eph. 5:27), it is at heart an instrument of God.

The Church makes possible my participation (in contemplation) in the events of Christ's earthly mission;

> that "opening" to heaven which he is, is like a gaping rent going right through humanity, and this rent is the Church. The fact that I, at this far-off spot in history, can be inserted into the reality of Christ by contemplation and discipleship, is something I owe to the reality of the Church.[15]

The Church is both the place of encounter with Christ, because of her liturgical prayer, and the realm of the Spirit, who is the medium of that encounter. The Church is founded by the sending of the Spirit, and it carries out its mission by con-

---

14. Balthasar, *Epilogue* (San Francisco: Ignatius Press, 2004), 44.
15. Balthasar, *Prayer*, 166.

tinually receiving the Spirit more deeply.[16] What it receives from the Spirit, it passes on to its members. The teaching office of the Church is not a concession to human weakness and sin but a vital aspect of its life in the Spirit.

For Balthasar, the Church can be called the "university of faith founded by the Holy Spirit."[17] It is a teaching Church, because teaching is a central part of training. In the sacraments of initiation (baptism, Eucharist, and confirmation), the Church is the "boot camp" for the members of God's earthly army. In its liturgy it is the continual training even the seasoned veteran needs. In its sacrament of reconciliation it is the medic. Bottom line: the Church is the army on Earth that one must join in order to carry out the mission.

DEPENDENCE ON GOD'S LOVE

I mentioned earlier that the person who encounters Christ and learns of his mission can respond with something other than, "Here I am Lord, your servant is listening" (1 Sam. 3:10). In fact, responding as Samuel did required both the Holy Spirit and Eli's prompting. Left to our devices and powers, we are sure to shrink from the call to arms. Conversion is hard work, and the only end of this labor is death—and it is not for the faint of heart. But it is also *not* something we must accomplish by our own power.

God is love, and he seeks from us a response of love. But human love cannot respond as it ought, because it is a limited and distracted love, even in those who will become saints. Only God's love is perfect. "God's love converts, transforms or

---

16. Balthasar, *Theo-Drama vol. III: Dramatis Personae* (San Francisco: Ignatius Press, 1992), 436.

17. Balthasar, *The Glory of the Lord vol. I: Seeing the Form* (San Francisco: Ignatius Press, 1982), 491.

hardens men's hearts but that is the effect, not the essence."[18]
The scandal is that God's love is so unlike anything we can
understand that we sometimes miss it and almost always misunderstand it. Continual growth in faith is required so that
one can respond each time the dialogue takes a new and more
serious turn. At each step along the way, God asks, "Do you
love me?" Each positive answer is a rung on the ladder to the
next challenge, the next manifestation of the call and the next
positive response.

The initial act of justification, which bestows a living faith,
is thus the model for all further acts in that continual exchange between God and man that is but the always living
union of the word by which God chooses man and the response by which man chooses God.[19]

Thus, it is not necessary to be blinded by God's extraordinary revelation of himself (like Saul on the road to Damas-
cus) to reap the grace needed for conversion. The underlying
model for each conversion experience (major or minor) is the
same. It is normally a gradual process, and one may not even
notice going from preparation for conversion to commission. (Although, at some point, there is always an initial and
decisive "Yes.") Along the way, every small act of obedience
leads to the ability to make greater acts of obedience.[20] God
transforms the world by transforming souls—and he does this
through everyday life. Scene by scene, God discloses to each
person the meaning of every stage of life as he sees it and as
he desires his disciple to see it.[21]

This learning to see as God sees is also being seen in the

18. Balthasar, *Love Alone* (London: Sheed & Ward, 1968), 58.
19. Balthasar, *The Christian State of Life*, 485.
20. Ibid., 489.
21. Balthasar, *Prayer*, 199–200.

light of Christ.[22] Often, when one first learns to see from this perspective, to see oneself as one really is, one does not like what is revealed. The answer "No" often arises as a result of this laying bare what man desired to remain hidden. This is at the heart of the center of gravity I mentioned earlier. It looks like a rejection of outside authority and the demands of discipleship. It is truly one's response to one's own sins.

When faced with the honest appraisal of one's identity before God, one can respond by desiring to change those aspects now seen as ugly. Alternatively, one can respond by rejecting the vision offered as untrue; and by extension, God is deemed unworthy of trust. Nothing but God's own light falls on us, but it can hurt if we have become accustomed to the darkness of sin.[23]

Why Conversion Is Rejected

In a culture where it is increasingly taboo to point out anyone's flaws or to engage in honest criticism, we tolerate our own defects by refusing to acknowledge them. Our culture reinforces this attitude by telling us everyone is special and, as at Lake Wobegon, "all the women are strong, all the men are good-looking, and all the children are above average."[24] Christ *does* fully reveal man to himself, but the resulting image is a burden to see.

The refusal of conversion (the answer "no") is also simple

---

22. Balthasar, *The Glory of the Lord vol. VII: Theology: The New Covenant* (San Francisco: Ignatius Press, 1990), 122.
23. Balthasar, *Prayer*, 236.
24. This quote originates with Garrison Keillor, in *A Prairie Home Companion*. More importantly, it is cited by Nan L. Maxwell and Jane S. Lopus in "The Lake Wobegon Effect in Student Self-Reported Data," *American Economic Review* (vol. 84, no. 2), May 1994, 201. The article uses the quote as the identifying name for trends of student self-reported data that serve to understate their deficiencies and overstate their achievements.

and complex. There are two supporting reasons why conversion is rejected. The first reason, and the most easily remedied, is that one does not understand divine love and sees only God's demand for repentance and obedience. Popular piety sees Christ as the carefree and loving guide to earthly happiness. He is the gentle and wise teacher who shows us how to live in harmony with each other. In this depiction, his harsh words are reserved for the Pharisees and the scribes, while prostitutes and sinners are welcomed with open arms.

For persons formed by this limited catechesis, the sound of God's call is no longer heard in its full power. "They regard it as something to be taken for granted, as something that does not require special attention.... It compels him to no conclusions that could force him out of the rut he is in."[25] We have already examined the many times in Scripture where Christ makes demands of his disciples and promises fire (of different types) for those who follow him as well as those who reject him. Overcoming an unbalanced notion of God's love is as simple as accepting the full gospel message rather than only those maxims that are comfortable. God accepts us as we are, but he also demands that we change.

The second supporting reason for the answer "No" usually is the interplay between human freedom and God's freedom. Balthasar called the misunderstanding of human freedom "Titanism." This is the idea that man is free, independent, and self-sufficient. Although man is certainly free (Adam and Eve taught us that much), the nature of that freedom is misunderstood. Christian freedom is first a freedom *for* what we were created to be and only secondarily a freedom *from* the effects of sin. One who suffers from Titanism rejects the need to find the fulfillment of human freedom in

25. Balthasar, *The Christian State of Life*, 427.

subordination to God. Modern man has turned from seeking true fulfillment to actually manufacturing fulfillment
where it does not exist.

The revelation of Christ made visible the abyss between
what man is and what he is called to be. Titanism turns away
from the abyss in horror and seeks to find another path that
does not require sacrifice and surrender. The "Lake Wobegon effect" impels man to build a monument to his own
achievements in the abyss, however false that monument may
be. Without grace, man is unable to even see the abyss that
separates him from God's vision of him, let alone cross it.
Confronted by the inability to be in true control of his own
destiny, man has responded by building and living in a destiny
manufactured by his own imagination.

Surrender of Control

This is why it is hard to be a disciple or an evangelist. We have
been seduced by the idea that we must be in control of our
destiny. We think we must shape our own future, when in reality we must let it go. For Balthasar, the answer "No" usually
begins with pretending not to hear the call of God. Of course,
this pretense means it has already been heard in some way.
Out of respect for human freedom, the light of divine glory
does not normally manifest itself in all its brilliance.[26] Because
the first call in the dialogue is usually a quiet call experienced
from within, it is too often ignored.

Rather than face the reality of a human life in need of
change (and the fact that human life is always already taken
up into the life of the Trinity), man retreats into his own humanity and seeks his comfort there. The danger involved in

26. Balthasar, *The Christian State of Life*, 427, 480.

conversion, the surrender of control, is spurned, and a happy resting place is manufactured to take its place.

Those persons with more natural talent and/or worldly success are more apt to choose such false comforts. Seeing their own strengths as entitlements rather than as gifts makes them unwilling to surrender for fear of losing those gifts.[27] This is why those who are less fortunate in life are often more ready to abandon themselves to God; the sick know they need a doctor, while the healthy are often unaware. Balthasar likens those who embrace such gifts rather than embracing the Gift-giver to those who refused to attend the king's banquet (see Matt. 22:2ff). The excuses those people gave were legitimate, but they reveal a fear of surrender to God and the unpredictable nature of the consequences of submission.[28]

Refusal does not obliterate personhood but disfigures it.[29] Out of respect for human freedom, God will leave us to the effects of our own bad decisions.

One who has ventured to look upon this love can perhaps act as though he has seen nothing, has heard nothing. He can hide behind the dictates of official morality and believe himself safe among men and perhaps even safe before God. But he deceives himself, for he will always be of the number of those who have said "no"; of those on whom Jesus has looked in sorrow.[30]

27. Ibid., 494.
28. Ibid., 495.
29. Balthasar, *Theo-Drama, III*, 266.
30. Balthasar, *The Christian State of Life*, 429.

Judgment

The effect of those bad decisions is judgment. In Balthasar's view, Jesus acts as judge not by handing down the sentence but by simply displaying the norm against which we judge ourselves.[31] If this is too passive a notion of judgment, perhaps it would be better to say that we have a hand in our own judgment, or that we are forced to judge ourselves and prevented from being less than honest. In our detailed look at conversion, we will see that the wrath of God was the other side of the coin of his fidelity to his covenant.

Likewise, the other side of salvation is judgment. If one rejects grace, "there is nothing left of the gift save judgment."[32] The Incarnation brings into history the possibility of a final "Yes" or "No." Christ carries in his person the demand for a decision. Once the Word is made flesh, sin is revealed as the final intensification of the "No" to God's Word.[33] Man's freedom of response is his entry to salvation or his doom.

God desires the response of faith, the childlike throwing of oneself into the arms of God, surrendering to the mission in each moment. Both Titanism and stripped down Christianity can be bars to this dialogue. "How many persons grow to adulthood in an atmosphere of unbelief or of lukewarm and liberal Catholicism without ever being exposed to the concept of a closer following of Christ?"[34] This closer following is the continual dialogue and the answer of "Yes" to the increasing demands which God puts before the human person.

31. Balthasar, *Does Jesus Know Us? Do We Know Him?* (San Francisco: Ignatius Press, 1984), 42.
32. Ibid., 81.
33. Balthasar, *Theo-Drama vol. IV: The Action* (San Francisco: Ignatius Press, 1994), 177.
34. Balthasar, *The Christian State of Life*, 496.

To do this, the Christian need not wait until his physical death, but he must begin to work at once; already in baptism he has died radically and had risen unto God, and he then spends the rest of his life training himself in this reality and living it out.[35]

Rejecting the call, and the resulting mission it imposes, is at least a missed opportunity. The individual is harmed, because he will no longer be able to be who he is meant to be, and the Church is harmed because of a mission not performed. No mission within the Church is given for the sole benefit of the person commissioned. The acceptance or rejection of a mission always has wider social implications.

> If one had accepted God's call, a vast multitude of one's fellow men might have gained access to the Lord; many who will now remain forever in their sins might have been drawn to confession; many who will now be left in ignorance might have accepted the word of God; many who will now be forever cold might have been inflamed by the fire of faith, hope and charity. As it is, a part of God's field will be forever uncultivated.[36]

The tragedy of refusing a call is not only the possible damnation of the individual but also the unknown negative effects on others. In our own day, the person who was to discover the cure to cancer may well have been conceived but aborted. Missions in the Church, which are given in dialogue with God, are by nature irreplaceable.[37]

---

35. Balthasar, *Seeing the Form*, 217.
36. Balthasar, *The Christian State of Life*, 497–498.
37. Ibid., 498.

3

EXECUTION

THE EXECUTION PARAGRAPH ADDRESSES HOW TO CARRY OUT THE MISSION AS IT RELATES TO THE FORCES, THE ENEMY, THE TERRAIN, AND OTHER DETAILS.

The mission statement may be slightly reworded here, so that the unit commander can emphasize different points, but it is always very close to the mission he himself has been given. Clarity, continuity, and brevity are essential for effective execution of the plan.

An important first part of the execution of any military operation is the preparatory fires. These can have several uses.

PREPARATORY FIRES

Most commonly, preparatory fires are used to kill the enemy or break his defenses. In general, they aim to make the main attack more effective by eliminating the numbers and types of enemy and weapons that can be brought to bear on subsequent forces. These fires by definition seek the enemy on his chosen ground and fight him there as opposed to maneuver, which seeks to hit the enemy where he isn't (or is weakest). In our case too they lay the groundwork for later success. Just as artillery and air power are used to knock down obstacles and defensive works, our "prep fires" seek to engage the enemy at a distance and render some of his arguments invalid.

Faith Is Reasonable

We begin with the proposition that faith is reasonable. We also begin with a definition of terms. One of the reasons dialogue aimed at conversion is either hard to come by or nonproductive is that defining one's terms is often neglected. When that happens, those in a dialogue will often speak past each other, since they conceive key terms in different ways. In this book, we will frequently employ the time-honored philosophical precept that one must first define one's terms. As you will learn, requiring definitions is a time-consuming affair. *Faith* is the first word we need to define, since it reveals (or conceals) a variety of shades of meaning. For now, I will keep it as simple as possible and define *faith* as "accepting as true something that, while one cannot prove it, has at least an internal certitude that invites acceptance." This is not blind faith, it is simply the way humans operate—it uses both reason and desire.

When we seek to show that faith is reasonable, we mean simply that it is not opposed to the proper use of grammar and logic and can be effectively proven or demonstrated by the rules of rhetoric. As previously stated, faith is not simply a matter of reasoned argument. As Blaise Pascal wrote, the heart has reasons that reason does not know. But at this stage we will focus on what reason can know.

Now that we have a working definition of faith, we will need to define some key terms within that definition. It may seem tedious, but if the immediate goal is understanding and the ultimate goal is conversion, we must take the time. Faith, in the sense I am using it thus far, is simply something we have used all our life and continue to employ on a regular (if not daily) basis. The way humans learn and how they go about the day's affairs is an interplay between faith and reason. Consider the following examples:

I am preparing for a family trip from Great Falls, Montana (my home) to Coeur d'Alene, Idaho. The travel trailer is packed and ready, and a happy Thanksgiving beckons at the end of our drive. The day before we are to leave, a weather system moves in. I check the projected road conditions and see that the passes over which I will be traveling will be covered in snow and ice. I make the prudent decision to cancel the trip, since I do not see the happy Thanksgiving with relatives as worth the cost (in gas and nerves—and possibly safety). This has been an exercise in faith and reason. I cannot prove that the road conditions will be as described by the weather forecast. I may even have a well-founded suspicion of the accuracy of the road predictions based on previous experience. Perhaps I don't even cancel the trip until I have checked the Internet site where I can view a scene via the cameras situated in Rodgers Pass and see for myself that the roads are in fact covered in snow and ice.

Does seeing the road conditions in real time constitute proof? That depends, again, on faith. Am I really seeing the road? I must have faith that the video being streamed over the Internet is actually showing the conditions in Rodgers Pass and is not some elaborate hoax concocted on a sound stage at the weather service. I must also make assumptions about my tow vehicle and trailer brakes. The only way I can actually prove that Rodgers Pass is or is not safe is to drive to the pass and attempt the climb (the easier part) and descent (the riskier part). Since I am not one of those people who consider the Apollo moon landings an elaborate hoax, I keep the family home and phone my regrets to my relatives in Coeur d'Alene. I suspect most people reading this would agree that I made a prudent and reasonable decision. Even those who might be inclined to see the decision as cowardly would not fault my reasoning process. In this case, faith was used in conjunction with reason to arrive at a decision.

Another example is doing homework with one of my children. My son was studying geometry and needed some help. The assignment was to work out geometric proofs for various problems. As my undergraduate degree (from twenty-some years ago) was in civil engineering, I set myself to guiding him through his geometry assignment, confident that my many years of mathematics would soon put any questions he had to rest. As we worked through the problems, I soon gained an appreciation of faith from a new perspective. Unable to work out which theorems applied and in what order to constitute a proof, I wanted to simply take on faith that lines and angles would have the properties I attributed to them. Working out the proofs was much harder than I had envisioned, since I had forgotten more geometry than I cared to admit.

As we learn mathematics (or biology or physics), we take certain things on faith. We trust that our textbooks and our teachers present things as they actually are. This trust is an exercise of faith. In this case we have no reason to believe that either the textbook or the teacher has intent to deceive. We know that parallel lines will never meet, because that is what our authority has told us. This form of faith is necessary to make progress in any academic discipline. As we progress in knowledge, what was once a matter of knowledge based on faith becomes a matter known by proof. Without taking some things on faith, we could not have made the progress necessary to arrive at the proof. (In the case of the geometry assignment, it remained faith until my son went back to school the next day and learned to work out the proofs his father could not.)

This example shows not only that faith is reasonable; it also shows that faith is necessary. Equally important, it shows that humility is a necessary condition for the proper application of faith and for reason to advance in knowledge. Humility about our limitations and trust in authority are keys to the advance of knowledge. As it is in these simple examples, so it is in more complex or esoteric forms of knowledge. All human knowledge is gained through interplay between faith and reason—trust in authority and the human desire to know on an ever more sure footing.

The Greek philosopher Aristotle said, "All men desire to know."[38] St. Thomas Aquinas pointed out that the proper object of the human intellect is truth.[39] Pontius Pilate asked, "What is truth?" (John 18:38). Eventually, we will look at all of these statements in more detail. At this point, it will suffice to point out that the advance of knowledge is a fragile and uncertain journey, though there are sure guideposts along the way. Trust in authority and honest humility about our lack of knowledge are keys to the advance of knowledge.

More About the Human Person

We need to return to our definitions (and we will), yet it is helpful to introduce another point. Our ability to use faith and reason together is central to our humanity. One can make little progress in describing how the human person does things without making some fundamental observations about the human person. Before examining what we know, it is necessary to examine how we know and what it means to know.

In the (supposed) Dark Ages of the sixth century, the philosopher Boethius wrote that the human person is a "ration-

38. Aristotle, *Metaphysics*, book 1, part I; http://classics.mit.edu/Aristotle/metaphysics.1.i.html.
39. Aquinas, *Summa Theologiae* I:16:1

al animal."[40] By this he meant that we are members of the animal kingdom. This unites us to a larger group of living things of which we are a part and is philosophical shorthand for saying that we hold many things in common with other members of this group. By adding the word *rational*, he is saying that what distinguishes us from other members of that group is our ability to use reason. This distinction was a more precise formulation of the observation of Aristotle that all men desire to know.

The nature of the human mind is that we have a drive to know things. This insatiable appetite may be more developed in some people than it is in others, but is present to some degree in all people. It is insatiable because we desire ultimate truth. It is insatiable also due to the nature of truth itself. The more we know, the more we develop other questions to which we simply must find answers. The unknown is an affront to our very nature, which impels us to an ever-deeper investigation that seeks to do away with mystery and replace it with knowledge. This is both the glory of the human being and a nagging frustration.

Certainly the modern advances in every field of human knowing have been an incredible testament to this human drive. At the same time they provide evidence of the insatiability. I read an article on the discovery of the Higgs boson by CERN (European Organization for Nuclear Research) at the Large Hadron Collider. The discovery has answered some of the nagging question in physics; it has also raised many more.[41] Such is the nature of science and, by extension, human knowing.

---

40. Boethius, *The Consolation of Philosophy*
41. Dennis Overbye, "Finding the Higgs Merely Opens More Puzzles," *New York Times*, Nov. 5, 2013, p. D1.

My point here is to lay down some basic principles in order to allow the original argument—that faith is reasonable—to proceed. Let us now return to my problem of defining terms within that first definition of faith. I wrote that faith is "accepting as true something that, while one cannot prove it, has at least an internal certitude that invites acceptance." In light of the open-ended nature of what the finite mind can know at any one point, one must "accept" certain things. What is meant by the word *accept*?

To accept something entails having sufficient confidence of the thing as true that one can proceed to further investigation. One does not simply "accept" but does so in a manner that allows for further investigation. Through further investigation, one may move from acceptance to certitude of truth. Of course, further investigation may lead to proof—or at least demonstration—that the thing initially accepted is *not* true. In that case, one must begin again without the accepted notion in light of the subsequent discovery of its lack of truth.

Again, such is the nature of human knowing and the necessity of humility. One must always be ready to question what one held as true in order to advance in knowledge. The interplay between faith and reason never ends. What changes are the particular notions that are accepted and acted upon or else are found unacceptable and therefore insufficient for further pursuit. The word *certitude* refers to the degree of reliability one attaches to a notion as a result of further investigation.

The interplay between faith and reason is constitutive of how the human person comes to know anything. This basic premise holds true in any field of human knowing, and, as we will see, it is tied to the nature of the human person. I am aware that there are more definitions yet to be expounded and more proofs or demonstrations yet to be developed—not the least of which is this thing I refer to as "human nature."

If I am careful, and the reader is patient, we will get to these things in their proper place.

Being Reasonable

I wish to move now the main question of this section of the chapter: is the Christian faith reasonable? Two things are necessary in asking this question. The first is describing what we mean by *reasonable*. The second, and more complex thing, is what we mean by *Christian faith*.

Reasonable means simply that the thing is open to investigation by the human intellect according to the rules of grammar and logic. *Grammar* refers to defining terms with clarity and precision and then using them in their proper sense. When a term has several shades of meaning, this entails using each form of the term accurately. A danger to dialogue is to define one particular form of a term and then use that same term in another sense without accounting for the change. Anyone who follows modern political discourse is aware of how terms can be abused in this manner. Formal logic, then, is necessary to ensure that, when we construct an argument, we are not confusing terms, definitions, and proper usage.

What I have described above is what was once known as the *trivium* of classical liberal arts education. Rather than complete the *trivium* before getting to the point, allow me one more short digression into logic.

A Short Lesson in Logic

The liberal arts take their name from the Christological statement, "You will know the truth, and the truth will set you free." The Latin word for free (*libero*) is the root of the word *liberal*. When the first universities were organized, they were a part of the Catholic Church, and the language of the Church was Latin. Not only was it the language of the Church, it was the language of scholarship. All the true liberal arts are aimed at the discovery of truth because the effect of truth is freedom.

The first course of studies in the medieval university was called the *trivium* and consisted of grammar, logic, and rhetoric. It was commonly understood that one could not proceed to any deeper form of knowledge in any area or discipline until one learned how to think. Grammar focused on the meaning and use of words; logic examined how to make a statement, and rhetoric put statements together to form an argument.

Watching the news or reading a paper, or the comments on a Facebook page—in varying degrees—offer proof that these topics have been neglected to the detriment of sound thinking.

The father of logical thought is widely held to be the Greek philosopher Aristotle. In the fourth century B.C., he set out the rules of formal and symbolic (aka mathematical) logic. Logic is defined as the science and art of evaluating and constructing arguments and systems of reasoning. A second definition you will need to be aware of is a proposition: a sentence or clause that makes a single statement that can be true or false. Finally, an argument is a string of related propositions that lead to a conclusion. In a good argument, the propositions are linked logically and build from the most evident to the point one is trying to make.

In an argument, there are two more key terms: *premise* and *conclusion*. A premise is a proposition that is the basis for the argument. In a valid argument, it needs to be recognized as true or previously demonstrated as true. A conclusion is a final proposition that follows by necessity from the premises.

For example:

Valid and true	Valid but false
Major premise: Socrates is a man.	*Major premise:* Mr. Incredible is a super.
Minor premise: All men are mortal.	*Minor premise:* All supers have special powers.
Conclusion: Socrates is mortal.	*Conclusion:* Mr. Incredible has special powers.

Note that an argument can be valid even if the premises are not true. There are no "supers" and no "special powers." The argument is valid, or logical, but because the premises are not true, the conclusion is false.

Logical Fallacies

In addition to errors of fact, an argument can be invalid for any number of reasons. Arguments that have factual errors are convincing only if one does not know the facts. This is common enough but also quite easy to overturn. More often, arguments that seem convincing are invalid because of logical fallacies, which are often referred to by their Latin names or their commonly used English equivalents:

- **Non sequitur:** Latin for "It does not follow." The conclusion does not follow necessarily from the premises. A common form of this is the *post hoc ergo propter hoc* ("after this, therefore because of this"), where the fact that one thing happens after another is held as proof that the first thing caused the second thing.

- **Burden of proof:** Maintaining that the burden of proof for an assertion lies not with the person making the claim but with someone else to disprove it.

- **Straw man**: Misrepresenting someone's argument to make it easier to attack (common in politics).

- **Ambiguity**: Using terms that have a range of meaning but restricting the meaning to a single one.

- **Begging the question**: Attempting to prove a conclusion with premises that assume that conclusion. (This phrase is often misused to mean "raising the question.")

- *Ad hominem*: Latin for "to the man." Attacking an opponent's character rather than his argument.

Popular Methods of Viewing "Knowledge"

There are two popular manners in which people approach knowledge that are logically invalid: subjectivism and scientism. Note that any time the suffix "-ism" is added to a word, it identifies an ideology.

Subjectivism holds that the truth or falsity of any given proposition is dependent solely on the person (or the "knowing subject"). Most people are selectively subjective. When faced with the proposition 2 + 2 = 4, they would not respond, "Well, that may be true for you, but it is not true for me." In other areas—especially in matters of faith—that is often their response.

Subjectivism is fatally flawed, because the word *true* means "corresponds to reality." There is only one reality, and it is not dependent on any knowing subject. It is also logically invalid because it assumes an objective truth: that all truth is subjective. Although most would not phrase it this way, subjectivism essentially claims that the only universally binding (or objective) truth is that there is no universally binding (or objective) truth. In other words, it is self-refuting.

To be fair, this type of thinking takes place when one cannot determine the truth of a given proposition. One of the tasks of theology is to clearly distinguish between what is known and what is believed. I hope you will find that there is actually far more known (provable or demonstrable) in theology than is simply "taken on faith."

The other popular invalid approach to knowledge is scientism. This is the view that the only things one can know to be true are those that can be proved or demonstrated using empirical data and the scientific method. Of course, the problem here is that it cannot be scientifically demonstrated that only the scientific methods can lead to truth—again, it is self-refuting. From a more practical perspective, when I say, "I love my wife," it can be true, but it cannot be scientifically proven.

Now, anything proved to be true by observation, measurement, and empirical data is really true—that is, not in question. The problem is, not all truths are open to this form of investigation. If that were the case, two millennia of philosophy would have been discarded with the onset of the scientific age—something no scientist ever argued for until the twentieth century.

Christian Faith

I began this section with a simple definition of faith. The more complex notion is the term *Christian faith*. The complexity of this term stems from many sources. The most obvious is that there are multiple Christian faith traditions that disagree on matters that pertain to how their adherents define "Christian." In seeking to get their arms around this term, many have tried to use some least-common-denominator form of Christianity. What "counts" as essential for being an adherent of the Christian faith? One common answer is the articles of faith contained in the ancient Nicene Creed (developed at the Council of Nicaea in A.D. 325). This approach has its benefits, but for now I wish to use an even more *de minimis* approach.

I do so not to call into question any of the articles of faith but because there are certain articles upon which others rest. In theology, we call this a hierarchy of truth. For example, demonstrating that the existence of God is reasonable is necessary before one can move on to a demonstration or proof about what that God has said, done, or requires of one who calls himself a Christian. That God exists is a higher truth upon which subsequent (or lower) truths necessarily rest. The second-century theologian Origen wrote a treatise called *On First Principles* as an attempt to capture the hierarchy of truths and some sense of certitude regarding them.

The Thomistic Approach

Among those who followed and built upon this foundation was Thomas Aquinas. He will be our primary guide throughout this section of the book. The format for much of St. Thomas's work follows something known as the scholastic method of theology. Simply put (perhaps too simply for some), this was a manner of Socratic dialogue by which the author poses a question and then seeks to answer the question. After stating the question, the author provides a series of objections to the question. These objections are what would have been the popular and/or academic positions held by those who did not agree with the answer the author is going to provide.

Following these objections, there would often follow some statement of authority, referred to in Latin as the *sed contra* ("on the contrary"). Since argument from authority (because an expert says so) is the weakest form of argument, it was not intended as an answer. It was instead a way of saying, "Perhaps there is a good reason to investigate the matter more closely."

There would then follow the author's answer to the question, or the *respondeo*. It is from these answers that I will draw Thomas's insights. Because the prose can be somewhat difficult for the contemporary reader, I will explain in common language what Aquinas was trying to say.

The question being treated would then close with a response to the objections which opened the question, applying the author's answer to the specific claims made in the objections. Occasionally it will be necessary to delve into these sections, because many of the objections offered today are the same ones Thomas had to address in a different form. A note of caution: most often, a single question might be broken into several parts. When one asks a complex question such as, "is it reasonable to believe that God exists?" it is often necessary to peel away the layers of questions inherent in the larger one.

As we move forward, I will be careful to distinguish between the logical categories of *proof* and *demonstration*. Different forms of knowledge are open to different forms of investigation. Some things can be proved (the highest form of knowledge), and others can only be demonstrated (a lesser form of knowledge). Although all forms of knowing are interplays between faith and reason, there are some matters we deal with in theology that will always remain matters of faith. In dealing with divine or supernatural notions, one can never move entirely beyond the level of *faith* as the term is more properly understood. The finite human mind is simply not able to solve some of the mysteries we will encounter. With the author of the Letter to the Hebrews, we must say, "Now faith is the assurance of things hoped for, the conviction of things not seen" (Heb. 11:1). If I do my job well, the reader will come to see that those things that must be taken on faith are few and that it is never a blind faith.

Our first question, then: Is it reasonable to believe that God exists? Since I am Irish, I will answer that question with another question: "Why is this the first question?" Since I am your guide, I will answer that for you. Because if God exists, then it logically follows that his existence has implications for us; if he does not exist, then there is no need for any further investigation.

This is an example of the hierarchy of truths, but it is also a critically important question to frame. Even a committed atheist, if he is honest, would agree that if this thing called "God" were actually to exist, a series of logical consequences would also exist. *What* these implications are would be dependent on the nature of God and humanity's relation to that God—all of which would require subsequent proofs or demonstrations of their own.

Once again, we see the necessity of faith in order for reason to work. For now, one must take on faith that the answer to the question "Does God exist?" has a series of further implications so that there is a logical reason to continue. Once existence is established, one can move on to what kind of a thing this God might be, what the human person is in relation to that God, and what follows from both of those notions.

As St. Thomas proposes (in *Summa Contra Gentiles*, book 1, chapter 4), the question of God's existence must be answered on two levels. There is a part that is accessible to human reason and a part that must be accepted as a matter of faith. This is so for two reasons.

One has to do with us. The human intellect is limited; we simply cannot know all that we would like to know about the existence and nature of God. There is incompatibility not just in scale but in kind: a finite mind cannot encompass the infinite. Even our language falls short of accurately expressing what we can know about God. This is a limitation our humility must accept.

The other reason has to do with God. If that term has any meaning whatsoever, it at least means a supernatural being or entity that by its very nature is beyond us. Now, if it seems that I am repeating myself, that is a demonstration of the importance of perspective and our limitation in language. The underlying limitation is the difference in nature between finite and infinite. This same limitation can be viewed as a function of us (from the finite toward the infinite) or as a function of the infinite (God) itself. If we could know God perfectly and completely, he would not be God; rather, he would be something that we can express and shape according to our own finite manner of knowing. One must always remember that we are made in his image and likeness, not the other way around. This is one danger to which even many committed Christians fall prey.

There is a further incidental complication. Although in general the finite intellect is not up to the challenge of the infinite, we are speaking here not about generalities but about actualities—actual people who are actually in the act of knowing. Once we get to that level, it is obvious that some actual finite minds are capable of a level of knowledge that will elude other finite minds.

Returning to St. Thomas, we see that, despite the complexity of the matter under investigation and the variation among human minds (and the time required to thoroughly investigate the intricacies and nuances), we are not without a remedy. That remedy is proportionate to us finite knowing subjects (in general) and as individual instance of finite minds (with the attendant strengths and weaknesses inherent in each instance). So, yes; we can have a reasoned faith.

The Preambles of Faith *(Praeambula Fidei)*

Before we tackle whether God exists, there are still more considerations—about us as humans and about the notion of God on which we must be clear. The nature of the human person is one who rebels at mystery and has a desire to know (SGC, ch. 5). This is evident in the history of humanity in general and in the history of philosophy in particular. The reason mysteries intrigue us is that they play off our basic nature as rational animals. When faced with mystery, the human intellect has an insatiable desire to solve it. Of course, there are people who, when faced with a mystery, shrug and return to their video game and Cheetos. My assumption is that you, dear reader, are not one of them—or at least not always.

Not only do we have a desire to know, we are equipped with an intellect that allows us to know. For all the previous talk about our finite limitations, we still possess the type of mind that is "fit" for the solving of mysteries and the attainment of knowledge. We can fail and we can achieve. Some will achieve a higher level than others, and all of us have to build on the great minds that have gone before us. Such is the manner in which we learn almost anything. Although taking things on faith is always an option, it is one that leaves us open to doubt. (Doubt as the flip-side of faith will be addressed later on.)

Aquinas coined the term "divine intelligibles" to describe something about the nature of our human intellect and something about God. Although St. Thomas had a high regard for the human intellect, he also understood its limitations. These limitations may be about particular instances of the human intellect or about the nature of the intellect in general. He even has a specific warning about those who, puffed up with pride about the abilities of the human mind, think they can know all things perfectly:

For there are those who rely on their own abilities to such an extent that they think that they are able to measure the whole nature of things by their own intellects—so that, namely, they consider true only what seems true to them and false only what does not seem true to them. So in order that the human mind, liberated from this presumption, might be able to attain to a modest investigation of the truth, it was necessary that God should propose to human beings things which altogether exceed their intellect.

For Thomas, man was not "the measure of all things." As I mentioned, the term "divine intelligibles" says something about God as well. He did create in such a manner as to reveal something about himself. But his nature is so far beyond our capacity to know that there are some things that must remain shrouded in mystery as well.

Two Types of Truth

In those things that we profess about God there are two types of truths. For there are some truths about God that exceed every capacity of human reason, such as that God is [both] three and one. But there are other truths that natural reason is also capable of arriving at, such as that God exists, that there is one God, and others of this sort. Indeed, philosophers, led by the light of natural reason, have proved these truths about God demonstratively (SCG, ch. 3).

Given these competing strengths and weaknesses, we proceed with a certain confidence and humility to ask if it is reasonable to believe that God exists. Does such a belief do violence to the nature of the human person? Or is it the result of using our intellect to examine the world (universe, cosmos) in which we live? Not surprisingly, a Catholic priest like Aquinas would answer no to the first question and yes to the second. He does so not from Sacred Scripture but from his exercise of human reason. His famous five demonstrations for the existence of God are well known (in certain circles) but misunderstood by many—sometimes by the same people at the same time. What follows will be an overview of them designed for those without advanced degrees in theology or philosophy. Far more will be omitted than included, but hopefully the reader can follow the basic arguments.

Infinite Regress

Three of the five demonstrations deal with the impossibility of infinite regress. More than a thousand years before Thomas took pen to hand, Aristotle pointed out that an infinite regression was not possible. If "this" depended on "that," the chain of "this" and "that" could not go on forever. At some point, there had to be a "this/that" that began the chain. Absent some beginning, the chain would never exist, but it is evident to everyone that the chain does exist. For example:

1. We have now shown that the effort to demonstrate the existence of God is not a vain one. We shall therefore proceed to set forth the arguments by which both philosophers and Catholic teachers have proved that God exists.

2. We shall first set forth the arguments by which Aristotle proceeds to prove that God exists. The aim of Aristotle is to do this in two ways, beginning with motion.

3. Of these ways the first is as follows. Everything that is moved is moved by another. That some things are in motion—for example, the sun—is evident from sense. Therefore, it is moved by something else that moves it. This mover is itself either moved or not moved. If it is not, we have reached our conclusion—namely, that we must posit some unmoved mover. This we call God. If it is moved, it is moved by another mover. We must, consequently, either proceed to infinity, or we must arrive at some unmoved mover. Now, it is not possible to proceed to infinity. Hence, we must posit some prime unmoved mover.

Although the example of the sun refers to physical movement, the term *motion* can be better thought of today as *change*, either in location or in state (ice melting and assuming a liquid form). Any motion or change has a cause. In the case of the melting ice, the cause is heat. The heat may be supplied by any number of sources, but for any given source of heat, there must be a further cause. In the case of the observed "movement" of the sun (obviously as seen from Earth), the motion is caused by the rotation of the Earth on its axis—even if Aristotle was unaware of the nature of the cause. But what causes Earth to rotate? Gravitational forces and the laws later discovered through physics. But what is the cause of those laws?

Generation and Corruption

Another form of the demonstration for the existence of God from reason alone concerns generation and corruption. Aquinas writes:

> We find in the world, furthermore, certain beings, those namely that are subject to generation and corruption, which can be and not-be. But what can be has a cause because, since it is equally related to two contraries, namely, being and non-being, it must be owing to some cause that being accrues to it. Now, as we have proved by the reasoning of Aristotle, one cannot proceed to infinity among causes. We must therefore posit something that is a necessary being. Every necessary being, however, either has the cause of its necessity in an outside source or, if it does not, it is necessary through itself. But one cannot proceed to infinity among necessary beings the cause of whose necessity lies in an outside source. We must therefore posit a first necessary being, which is necessary through itself. This is God, since, as we have shown, he is the first cause. God, therefore, is eternal, since whatever is necessary through itself is eternal.[42]

The simplest example is *you*. You came to be through the action of your mother and father. Even if some artificial means were employed, you at least needed a human egg and a human sperm. Each of your parents was similarly dependent on parents and so on. Although this is the simplest example, it is not the only one. Everything we know in nature, the universe, the cosmos; comes into being and passes out of being. And

42. Aquinas, *Summa Contra Gentiles* I:15

yet something that does not exist cannot bring itself into existence. We speak of the "birth" and "death" of stars and even entire galaxies; they come into being and at some time they will cease to be. If infinite regress is not possible, then there must be a necessary and eternal cause. One need not posit the Christian God as that cause, but one must admit there is a cause, because logic compels it.

The latest versions of the multiverse theory hold that there are multiple universes, each with its own set of physical laws. To say these universes come into being and pass out of being from each other is still an attempt to point to a cause of things that come into being. Here we enter a modern phase of the question Aquinas commented on in his more well-known work, the *Summa Theologiae*.

Governance

The fifth way is taken from the governance of the world. We see that things which lack intelligence, such as natural bodies, act for an end, and this is evident from their acting always, or nearly always, in the same way, so as to obtain the best result. Hence it is plain that not fortuitously, but designedly, do they achieve their end. Now whatever lacks intelligence cannot move toward an end, unless it is directed by some being endowed with knowledge and intelligence; as the arrow is shot to its mark by the archer. Therefore some intelligent being exists by whom all natural things are directed to their end; and this being we call God.

Whether considering the universe, or multiple universes, or the behavior of subatomic particles, physics discovers laws that govern (in most cases) how parts of nature act or interact. These laws are what Aquinas would refer to as instances of natural bodies acting "always or nearly always, in the same way, so as to obtain the best result." Had he been aware of the scientific advances of our day, he would no doubt have added more specificity to his argument, but the basic premise remains unshaken. What explains why the laws of physics are as they are? Even if there are multiple universes that arise out of each other, each having its own unique physical laws, the fact that each has laws that govern its structure, existence, and action would be evidence of some form of intelligent activity.

Earlier I mentioned that, without sufficient definition of terms, adversaries in an argument tend to speak past each other. The physicist can describe laws, but the philosopher or theologian asks why there are laws at all. Physicist Stephen Hawking's latest theory is that multiple universes—in theory an infinite number of them, each with their own unique sets of laws—create each other. Therefore, Hawking claims, they were created out of nothing. If he had read either Aquinas or Augustine of Hippo, he would have found that *creatio ex nihilio* has long been the Christian position.

The modern versions of this argument are far more complex than what I have presented here, but a fundamental disconnect remains. Empirical science, because it is limited by its own method, seeks to explain how more than why. Once the step is taken from how to why, one has ceased to deal with observable or experimental phenomena subject to verification or falsification.

"Why?"

The question "why" has long been the province of philosophy and theology, because it is a metaphysical question. Metaphysics, as the name implies, uses information (data, observation, experimentation) from the physical realm to go beyond what can be observed or measured. An interesting trend in modern physics is the increasing degree to which it is parallel to some of the most basic questions posed by philosophy and theology. Hawking arrives at *creatio ex nihilio* just as the ancient Christians did—though by that term they signify different things. Similarly, the search for the Higgs boson is essentially an attempt to explain why there is something rather than nothing—a question that plagued the men of Athens hundreds of years before the birth of Jesus the Nazarene.

Faith and reason are not in opposition; they are complementary. Modern physics and theology are not at war with one another; they have different ways of approaching their questions. The more one delves into the matter, the more confluence—or possible confluence—one finds, so long as one has not excluded any particular approach at the outset. The details of the arguments may be worlds apart, but the basic questions may be quite similar. The human person wants to know, and he wants to know more than just "how"—he wants to know "why." As long as this insatiable human drive to know both how and why remains, the seemingly disparate disciplines will need to find a way to get along with each other.

Faith, then, is—at the very least—reasonable. Actual faith is a gift but one shared by every people in every culture and every age. This does not prove faith (or why would there be a need); it only shows it is not a delusion and not opposed to how our minds work.

MAIN ATTACK: ENCOUNTER WITH CHRIST

In military operations, the execution part of the orders is a list of detailed tasks for each subordinate unit and timelines for achieving those tasks. When the enemy is using nonconventional tactics, however, a simple list of tasks to be accomplished is not enough. In asymmetrical warfare such as we

face here, something called "mission-type orders" are employed. Mission-type orders strive to give the subordinate
unit leaders a deep understanding of the mission so that they
can adapt to the situations in which they find themselves. The
goal is to provide the necessary vision for the end goal and
allow maximum flexibility as to how to accomplish that goal
by responding to the situation as it is experienced. This will
be our approach here.

Recall that our objective is to get souls to heaven. Our
scheme of maneuver is conversion by encounter with Christ.
If one is fully informed as to what the encounter with Christ
looks like, then one can help bring this encounter about in a
manner fit for the particular situation. In this section we focus
on encounter as dialogue. Each target (potential convert or
revert) must be led to an encounter with the risen Lord in a
manner fit for that person. Here the meeting of the person
with the action of the Holy Spirit will accomplish the objective. The Christian soldier must be aware that the primary
actor in the encounter will be God and that the soldier need
only play that part given to him and trust that the matter lies
in the more capable hands of the divine Three in One.

There are some who can be swayed by logical argument
and others who will be moved by beauty or goodness. Eventually, the whole person must be engaged; the heart as well
as the mind must be moved. This movement cannot come
about through force of argument or coercion. If, as we noted,
people are prone to rebel at what they see as an imposition
from the outside, then dialogue must facilitate an encounter
that these people can enter into and experience from within.
Our guide in this section will once again be Hans Urs von
Balthasar, the late Swiss-German Jesuit. He sees conversion as
a dialogue centered on the acceptance of a mission that God
has prepared and reserved for each person. This Christian

mission—the enrollment in God's army—is nothing other than a portion of the mission of the Redeemer. Each person has a share in that mission, and conversion is the process of discovering and embracing that mission.

> "What do you seek?" The Lord does not immediately say: "Come and see!" That would be dictatorial and would do violence to the seekers, even if it were what they themselves wanted. Nor does he ask: "Do you want to come to me?" That would make it too easy for them, and he must leave open the possibility that they are seeking something else. God's question is a facilitating invitation, which, however, does not prejudice the human answer.[43]

Conversion Is a Dialogue

Conversion is an ongoing dialogue between God and man. When man encounters God, he encounters beauty; and, in Balthasar's thought, beauty always elicits a response from the beholder. But his concern is that this approach may result in seeing God and man not just as partners in dialogue but as equal partners. Man may come to be understood as having certain claims on God. For Balthasar, such a situation is unacceptable.

The Christian revelation cannot be reduced to a system based on the principle of dialogue. Even though the individual may adapt language creatively to his own personality—it remains a common medium. Between man and God, however, the only language possible is the word of God, that is if we mean a genuine, personal disclosure, and not some vague

---

43. Balthasar, *The Grain of Wheat*, Erasmo Leiva-Merkakis, translator (San Francisco: Ignatius Press, 1995), 42.

knowledge of one another's existence; and this communication is only possible if it so pleases God to make his word understood by man, which means to say, if he interprets himself in speaking to man.[44]

I will ensure that this analysis of conversion does not fall into such an error. At the same time, considering theological topics through the motif of dialogue is almost unavoidable, given the Christian understanding of Jesus as Word (Gr., *logos*) and the Holy Spirit who interprets our prayers to God (see Rom. 8:26).

In this dialogue of encounter, there are two possible responses: the "yes" of conversion and the "no" made possible by man's free will. Both responses are made possible by God. Grace not only calls for conversion, it carries with it the ability to respond affirmatively. The effects of sin and human freedom make the "No" response possible.

The dialogue between God and man began as myth. Prior to God's revelation of himself in Christ, man sought to explain his relationship to the cosmos and his own self-understanding by way of myth. It was his way of capturing a truth that was inescapable but that he did not yet see clearly.

The next stage of the dialogue was found in philosophy. Here again, man ponders his connections to the cosmos and himself, as well as the meaning of those connections. The fundamental philosophical investigations—the One and the many, Being and nonbeing, essence and existence—are at their core theological. Answers provided by pagan philosophy were only intermediaries; they needed their fullness in the revelation of God.

Once overtaken by theology, philosophy's shortcomings are laid bare. Because philosophy is concerned with knowl-

---

44. Balthasar, *Love Alone*, 39.

edge rather than love, it cannot answer the questions posed by the human person. The human person is always an object of love (God's love) and ordered toward love. Where philosophy sought knowledge, love seeks conversion. "God's love or *agape* answered the questions that had been heretofore beyond the reach of philosophy. And the answer appeared not as wisdom but as a call to conversion."[45]

The preliminary stages of dialogue found in myth and philosophy were incomplete because they did not yet have access to the complete Word of the Creator. Just as in human discourse the intelligibility of a sentence is not fully known before the final syllable has been spoken,[46] man's search for meaning could not find a definitive answer before Christ. In the beginning, man acted in Adam; in the fullness of time, God acted in Christ. The result continually unfolds as a dialogue between creature and Creator as the former struggles to provide a response to the latter.

Christ as God's Word to Man

Christ is the Father's Word to humanity. The Father speaks in his Son, and no one can come to the Father except through the Son. The dialogue between the human person and God is always primarily Christological, but because no member of the Trinity operates alone, dialogue is also always Trinitarian. The dialogue of conversion is no different.

To say that grace is Christological means something more than that it is caused by the merit of Christ. In grace, the

45. Balthasar, *Love Alone*, 11.
46. Balthasar, *Does Jesus Know Us? Do We Know Him?*, 89. "A melody [or sentence] is never properly understood until the last note [syllable] has died away. Then the original unity is reassembled by the hearer; similarly one can only understand the Cross from the perspective of Easter."

Trinity addresses the individual believer personally; and the believer is one only because he has received a share in the life of Christ as a member of his body, and in the measure accorded him (not quantitative, of course, but qualitative) by the Holy Spirit (Rom. 12:3, 2 Cor. 10:13, Eph. 4:7).[47]

The Trinitarian nature of the dialogue is exemplified by the speech of St. Peter on Pentecost (see Acts 2:5ff). Peter's speech is about Christ, but he speaks with words given him by the Holy Spirit. Importantly, it is the Spirit operating within the members of the crowd that enables them to hear Peter's words in their native tongues. This scene, while powerfully displaying the power of the Holy Spirit, nonetheless highlights the freedom of the human person in the dialogue.

In the twenty-first century, we are back in first-century Jerusalem. The New Evangelization can be nothing other than the original one played out on a contemporary stage. For some in the crowd, the reaction is astonishment followed by the question, "What does this mean?" (Acts 2:12). The Holy Spirit interprets Peter's words to them, and their response is one of openness and astonishment. They cannot yet react as Mary did, where, despite her confusion, she responded with, "Let it be done to me according to your word" (Luke 1:38). Her receptivity to the Spirit is pure and complete. For those in the crowd at Pentecost, the response falls short, but it remains a free human response, and it remains open to continued dialogue.

Others in the crowd are not so open. They have the same experience of the Holy Spirit, and they hear the words, but their reaction is closed and finite. They see only the possibility of an earthly explanation for the spectacle before them— "They have had too much new wine" (Acts 2:13). Despite

47. Balthasar, *A Theology of History* (San Francisco: Ignatius Press, 1994), 68.

the fact that these men were on a religious pilgrimage and no doubt aware of their own history as the chosen people, they cannot entertain the thought that God might once again be acting in their midst. Focused on the finite, they place the responsibility for the phenomenon on Peter and the other apostles: it must be drunkenness.

Those in the crowd who are open to the promptings of the Spirit ask Peter what they ought to do. They trust him to direct them according to God's will. Peter tells them to repent and be baptized, revealing God's appointed way to enter into a new relationship with him; in other words, Peter calls them to conversion.

In keeping with Jewish tradition, they must first be cleansed. Then, through the sacrament administered by the nascent Church, they will begin a new relationship with God. In the conversion of the 3,000, one can see all the elements of the dialogue in play: the centrality of Christ, the role of the Holy Spirit, the example of Mary, and the role of the Church are established at the very beginning.

A second motif is also at work in this scene. There are those in the crowd who respond to Peter with a "no." It is easy to see how Peter's speech would have caused offense to many in the crowd. It is a natural human reaction to respond to criticism with hostility. Today there are many who have rejected faith or the Church because they have been challenged by someone's preaching. Peter, following his Master's example (see John 6:60ff), allows his message to be rejected. Just as the dialogue partner must be open to continuing the conversation, today's Christian troops must be open to rejection. Pope Benedict XVI advised those seeking to witness to the faith (speaking to the bishops) to expect to be beaten.[48] The

48. Benedict XVI, "Homily for the Feast of the Epiphany," 2013.

wisdom of this age will meet the call to faith with derision, just as it did in Jerusalem. The modern spiritual combat is not for the faint of heart.

Those who reject the call to conversion are either closed to divine interaction or shocked by the radical nature of the call. As we will show later, there is a third possible response: "Maybe" or "Yes, but." It is easy enough to imagine there were those present at Pentecost who responded in such a manner.

The negative response to God, whatever form it takes, is a perfectly understandable human response. It is only the grace of Christ that allows the human person to respond in the positive. Only God's love given to man in Christ enables him to utter a response fitting for God.[49] Christ carries with him both the possibility of answering in love and the judgment that results from the answer of "No." Without the aid of grace, the human response is only human. For most of those in the crowd that day, the expected response would be some form of rejection of Peter's words. The inspiration of the Holy Spirit is what makes the difference. He brings the apostles out of hiding in a dramatic fashion. He is the one who speaks within the human person and gives him the ability to hear and then accept the startling message. It is the grace of Christ, made active in the hearer by the Holy Spirit, that overcomes the merely human response. The Holy Spirit is now manifest as the Spirit of the risen Lord, and he carries out the continuation of Christ's mission in the world.

The pattern one sees at Pentecost began within the apostles, during the life of Christ and after the Resurrection. During his earthly ministry, even Christ's own disciples are unable to see clearly the full meaning of the teaching they

---

49. Balthasar, *Convergences: To the Source of Christian Mystery* (San Francisco: Ignatius Press, 1983), 95.

received. With their leader broken, bloodied, and dead, the disciples were scattered and broken themselves. They even return to their former way of life as fishermen. Their encounter with the resurrected Christ and his subsequent teaching begin to show them the continuity of his message beyond the discontinuity of his death. Balthasar says:

> The Word of God first speaks, then suffers, dies and rises in the end. Only the three syllables together make up the whole Word, which God addresses to us in Christ. The first syllable by itself [the earthly preaching] could not be comprehended by the disciples.[50]

This was why the risen Christ stayed with his disciples for forty days after the Resurrection—so that they might see the continuity between his mission and death. He comes to them repeatedly to open their eyes and explain to them how the crucifixion was a necessary part of his work rather than the end of it. Even then, they require the inspiration of the Holy Spirit at Pentecost to finally embrace their mission. The Holy Spirit allows them to see the place their mission has in relation to Christ's and to follow their missions to their own glorious ends. For each person in history, the key to the dialogue is in seeing one's mission as being taken up into the mission of Christ. The human person must see the part he or she is called to play as an extension of Christ's mission from the Father.

The Holy Spirit as Interpreter and Response

The Holy Spirit plays a critical role in the human response in the dialogue of salvation and faith. The work of the Holy

---

50. Balthasar, *Test Everything: Hold Fast to What is Good*, 87.

Spirit in conversion is at once powerful and understated. It is the Spirit who brings life to the message of Christ within the human heart, and yet Spirit never draws attention to himself. Within the Trinity, he is the bond between the Father and the Son. He continually serves to point away from himself and toward the other divine Persons. In the work of salvation, he similarly brings Christ alive in people (and in the Church) and allows their lives to follow the same path as the Savior.[51] He orients the believer toward Christ, who in turn brings him or her to the Father. Each disciple of Christ is required to undergo this transfiguration from the death of sin to a new life in Christ.[52] These transfigurations are the work of the Holy Spirit, who is the power *by* which they occur as well as the milieu *in* which they occur. It is he who realizes the work of the Father and the Son in the world, in the Church, and in each individual heart.[53]

The Weight of the Call

The Father calls the human person by the Word, who is his Son. The human person cannot bear to look upon the Father's face (see Exod. 33:20), so we are given the divine-human face of the Son upon whom we may look and with whom we can enter the dialogue. This divine-human face of the Son, and the words he speaks, seek to bring the human person to the Father by degrees. He conceals the full light of the Father's glory:

> Divine love may give itself with such overwhelming power that man perceives nothing but the crushing majesty of the

---

51. Balthasar, *Theology of History*, 80, 98. See also, *Seeing the Form*, 512.
52. Balthasar, *Mysterium Paschalae*, 204.
53. Ibid., 131.

Glory, and his response is concentrated into a single answer, utter obedience; but both the word and answer derive their meaning from the fact that the eternal Person has given himself a finite person in such a way that the possible answer is included in the very act of giving, whose heart and essence is love.[54]

Because the power of this vision is indeed crushing, it is not normally the beginning of the call to conversion but the culmination. The dialogue the Father establishes through his Son is meant to slowly accustom man to the fullness of the glory to be revealed in him when he is finally united with the Father. In order to see the Father's call as one of love, the finite creature needs a measured approach so that he might be attuned to the fullness that awaits him. The modern evangelist must also be conscious of the weight that conversion bears and be equally gentle in seeking to bring it about. Pushing too hard or too fast may turn a person away from the Faith and leave him more estranged than when the dialogue began.

The Human Response

All who are brought to an encounter with Christ are faced with the decision to surrender and follow or to rebel. Conversion is the choice to surrender and follow, but it is also a gift of grace. It is a gift that remains to be embraced by every person. Conversion is the lifelong dialogue between God and the Christian that accounts for human weakness and freedom. It is a continual "Yes" to the offer of grace (which overcomes weakness) and the full flowering of human freedom.[55]

54. Balthasar, *Love Alone*, 47–48.
55. Ibid., 119.

It was remarked earlier that the role of the Holy Spirit is instrumental in the human response of "Yes" to God. In order to understand the continual "Yes" of the human person under grace, it is necessary to ask, "Who (or what) is the human person in whom the Holy Spirit seeks to make the transformation?" Man is a creature who exists over time. I am not today all I will be twenty years or even twenty minutes from now. The key for Balthasar is that man exists in dialogue and tension with the future—"everything that exists is a 'not yet' of what it can be, ought to be, perhaps will be."[56] In light of this tension between what the human person is and what he is called to be in Christ, one's mission is to be always open to the guidance of the Holy Spirit. When the Spirit places before man the Father's will, man is called to follow wherever the Spirit leads. This docility to the Spirit is the true measure of human freedom, exactly as it was Christ's freedom to do the will of the One who sent him.

Fallen man cannot assume his mission in any way aside from the indwelling of the Holy Spirit. Each believer must be changed and become more like Christ. It is the Holy Spirit who effects the change. The goal of the modern warrior is to bring people to this transformation and then step back and let the Holy Spirit take over. The indispensable means of enabling this dialogue of encounter is prayer. Prayer is the place of encounter and dialogue that initiates, guides, and completes the transformation in Christ. So the warrior must himself be a man of prayer who can show others what it means to pray.

The Spirit is able to take our weak acts of prayer and lift them up so that they become pleasing to the Father.[57] He is

---

56. Balthasar, *Explorations in Theology: vol. III: Creator Spirit* (San Francisco: Ignatius Press, 1993), 135.
57. Balthasar, *Prayer*, 76.

able to be our "translator," because he experienced the human state in the person of Christ[58] and knows how to speak like us. Because he is God, he is eternally in dialogue with the Father and the Son. Seen from this perspective, the dialogue of prayer is synonymous with the Trinitarian exchange of love.[59] Whereas the Holy Spirit *is* what he *does*, man *becomes* what he does; he becomes Christ-like only by docility to the Spirit, and this is normally accomplished in prayer.

So what exactly happens in prayer? Balthasar considers the conversion of a person as the burning away of sin in the soul, which explains why the Holy Spirit appeared as tongues of flame at Pentecost. He is the fire that Christ came to light (see Luke 12:49) and the baptism of fire foretold by John the Baptist.[60] Prayer produces an attitude of being open to the action of the Holy Spirit. Openness to the Spirit, and to grace,[61] gives to man the eyes and ears of faith (see Matt. 13:43). These spiritual qualities allow him to see the depth and fullness that lies beyond his sense organs; he learns to "see" and "hear" (and taste and feel) contemplatively.

The pattern of a continual call and a continual response that becomes increasingly more serious played out in the life of Christ as well. Christ, having set aside divine foreknowledge of his own mission, continually responded to the Father's will as set before him by the Spirit. The drama of Gethsemane (see Matt. 20:22) reveals the challenge of drinking the cup to its last dregs and following the Father's will to the end. For Christ, as for Peter, the call to conversion (or obedience to the Father's will) becomes ever deeper and costly. The dialogue

---

58. Balthasar, *Creator Spirit*, 123.
59. Ibid., 179.
60. Balthasar, *Theo-Drama, IV*, 60.
61. Ibid., 112.

leads to a deeper intimacy with God by offering a greater challenge and demanding the continual "Yes."

Too often this dynamic is missing in prayer. Many Christians consider prayer to be a human initiative wherein they express their praise, desires, or concerns to God and await a response. But prayer is always a dialogue wherein God speaks first and the human person responds.[62] Until one can learn to see prayer in this way, one will never really hear or discover how to respond.[63]

Once that realization is achieved, one understands that the Incarnation, death, and Resurrection of Christ occurred for each individual person as though no other person existed. Once someone understands this action as taking place for oneself, one cannot be passive. This is Balthasar's understanding of prayer: the essential thing is to come face to face with truth, goodness, and beauty and be transformed by it.[64]

The transformation wrought by entering into this type of prayer is self-emptying love. The Father empties himself (pours out all that he is) in the generation of the Son. The Son empties himself in both the Incarnation and in his Passion. The only fitting response is a human self-emptying. "And since the only reason I owe my whole being to him is because he sacrificed his being for mine, the only way to express my thanks is with my whole being."[65] Balthasar calls the Passion of Christ a visual aid to our knowledge of God.[66] When we understand God as self-emptying love, we can begin to respond to God's initiative in the same way and become the theological person God envisioned at the moment of cre-

62. Balthasar, *Creator Spirit*, 32.

63. Balthasar, *Prayer*, 15.

64. Ibid., 305–306.

65. Balthasar, *The Moment of Christian Witness* (San Francisco: Ignatius Press, 1994), 24.

66. Balthasar, *Does Jesus Know Us? Do We Know Him?*, 78.

ation. For Balthasar, "The essence of being a Christian is to be open daily and hourly to the call of God and to let oneself be touched and guided by it."[67]

OBSTACLE-BREACHING PLAN

In a military operations order, the obstacle-breaching plan shows how the attacking force intends to deal with the obstacles identified in the intelligence part of the order (specifically, in the terrain and obstacle analysis). It is set off in its own section so that it is clear to the reader that it is merely a supporting operation. It may be absolutely necessary in order for the main attack to succeed, but it should not become the focus. The commander wants his units focused on the main attack. (Of course, the subordinate unit tasked with actually destroying or reducing an obstacle does become entirely focused on that mission.)

As you have seen, the main attack is the encounter with Christ. In that section and in the prep fires section we dealt with some of the obstacles arrayed against us. This section of the order contains additional and amplifying information about how to overcome more of these obstacles. In some cases, they will be obstacles already addressed. As we saw in the prep fires section, there are times when other measures have not accomplished all that they were meant to accomplish. At least for now, imagine that your mission is to tackle one of the obstacles previously identified.

The obstacle-breaching plan has three main components:

1. Identify/locate the obstacle (see *Situation: Intelligence: Terrain and Obstacle Analysis*).

---

67. Balthasar, *The Christian State of Life*, 435.

2. Cover it by fire.

3. Reduce or bypass the obstacle.

To "cover it by fire" means to shoot at the enemy forces present at or controlling the obstacle so that they cannot focus on their own mission of stopping the approaching force. Sometimes this is all that is needed to render the obstacle ineffective. There are some obstacles that can be defeated simply by explaining why one need have no fear of them. The obstacle will still be present, but it will be ineffective. In fact, two of the most common obstacles are of this sort.

To "reduce" an obstacle usually means to destroy it. To bypass it is to simply choose another route of advance. Since many obstacles are of a stationary nature, this is often the most efficient choice. But there are times where the terrain dictates areas where a force must move, and if the enemy is smart (and ours is), he has placed them where they cannot be avoided. This is the situation we face; there is really only one avenue of advance open to us. St. Matthew tells us:

> Enter by the narrow gate; for the gate is wide and the way is easy, that leads to destruction, and those who enter by it are many. For the gate is narrow and the way is hard, that leads to life, and those who find it are few (Matt. 7:13-14).

Because we are given only this avenue of advance, we must attack some obstacles directly.

Natural Physical and Moral Laws

The first of these more serious obstacles that must be reduced is the notion that God does not exist. Although this was addressed as part of prep fires, every good soldier knows that the prep fires never accomplish all that one hopes they would. In our case, we will present a second set of arguments to be used in case the ones in the prep fires section were not effective. Until this idea is overcome, there is no possibility of moving forward. Perhaps it would be better to say that one cannot move forward until one has at least begun to reduce this obstacle. It may well be the case that there are other obstacles connected to this one. Any wise enemy would ensure that his obstacles are interconnected and mutually supporting.

In the broadest sense, it seems that there is at least some evidence that something one can call "god" exists. Every culture known to man has had some form of religious belief, some concept that the material and visible world is not all there is to reality, some notion of God. In some cases it was a nature god, and in other cases there were multiple gods. Although there is strong evidence that there have always been those who have not embraced their culture's religion, they have been (and still are today) a distinct minority.

This universality of religion makes it a part of what is known as the natural law. Natural law is often defined as "things we can't not know." This is a simple definition and not an entirely accurate one. It would be better to say that the natural law consists of those things that, once investigated or explained, one realizes must be the case.

The easiest natural laws to understand are those that have been confirmed by modern empirical science—the laws of physics or biology are examples. They are binding on all of creation and everywhere. Certainly there are exceptions to things like the law of gravity—think of outer space or of artificially created conditions of weightlessness. But even though the phenomenon of zero gravity can exist or be created, there is no doubt that the force of gravity is a fundamental building block of the cosmos; without it there would be chaos rather than cosmos. It is a "first principle" upon which everything else is built. Natural laws are not ironclad, but they are foundational. They can be violated but cannot be nonexistent.

Natural laws that are not subject to the examination by the physical sciences are more problematic in convincing the unbeliever. There are natural moral laws. These are things that every culture has recognized throughout time, albeit in different forms. The ancient Greek philosopher Aristotle reflected on the existence of such natural laws. In his *Ethics*, he points out that travel was the best way to determine if something people did (or failed to do) was a natural law or a mere culturally specific custom. Once an Athenian traveled to Carthage and saw people acting in a manner different than people in Athens, he would understand that certain practices of the Athenians were culturally conditioned norms and not natural laws. He would also see that, for all the differences, there were also commonalities. If one were to travel to enough places, one could begin to formulate the natural moral or social laws. Of course, no one could travel as extensively as would be necessary to make such a determination. What we can do today is study other cultures and times and come to an understanding about what these universal social phenomena are or have been.

From the Judeo-Christian perspective, one can note that most of the Ten Commandments are natural moral laws. Although Yahweh revealed the prohibition of murder, lying, and stealing to Moses on Mount Sinai, it was not the case that the world had never known these prohibitions before. Nor was the Golden Rule an invention of the ancient Israelites. Nearly every major world religion has some form of the idea that one ought to treat other people in the manner in which one wants or expects to be treated.

The fact that so many religions have given voice to these

natural moral laws is at least an indication that they belong to the human race by virtue of what it means to be human. That they are placed in a religious context is equally important. The link between the natural law and our status as human beings will be developed further as we explore something called "Christian anthropology"; for now we can at least say that the natural moral law appears to be a universal concept. There is disagreement as to what constitutes the natural moral law, but there can be little doubt that it exists.

Realities Beyond What We Can See

Religion, then, is one of those universals; we don't recognize it as easily as we do the laws of physics, but it is recognizable nonetheless. The Christian would find that the natural moral laws are those that St. Paul says are "written on the heart" by God. They are a part of what makes the human animal different from any other animal and at the same time part of our human nature.

In recent years there have been many attempts to explain the universality of religion from a nonreligious (or antireligious) perspective. The phenomenon exists and requires an explanation; what that explanation is depends largely on the perspective of the one doing the explaining. Ever since the Age of the Enlightenment there have been philosophers or commentators who have predicted that as man becomes more scientific and sophisticated he will eventually "outgrow" religion. For as long as the prediction has been made it has been simultaneously disproven. This lack of experiential proof of the hypothesis (religion as superstition or a phase of evolution) has not stopped people from proposing it anew with new explanations.

There are those who claim religion can be explained by a

"God gene"—that the human animal is controlled by a specific gene or gene sequence to have religious belief. Others see it as a mere epi-phenomenon caused by a combination of chemical and electrical activities in the brain. Still others point to religion as serving a beneficial evolutionary function. Some see it as superstition or a reaction to areas of knowledge not yet sufficiently developed. Although this is not an exhaustive list of explanations given by nonbelievers, it is representative of the major views.

Two things are lacking in these explanations. First, they are unproven—many of them claim to be based in science, yet they fail the methods of science. The hypothesis can be stated and the conditions of the experiment defined, but the scientific confirmation always fails. Second, the investigation into religion is done with the assumption that it cannot be that religion is real (called an *a priori* bias). The one thing ruled out before the investigation begins is that religion is a response to a God or gods.

Note that I call it a believing-based examination and not a Christian-based one—we will get there, but not yet. For a religious adherent, there is an understanding that there are realities beyond what we can sense or otherwise measure. More importantly, this unseen and un-sensed reality forms the basis for what we *can* sense. Just as in my example about gravity, the uncreated and eternal realities of religion are "necessary" or foundational to all that we can know or sense. *The unseen undergirds and explains all that is seen.* This is the most broad and fundamental definition of religion. It cannot be proven by any empirical or even theoretical science, because those sciences themselves depend on the very laws established by the divine. By definition, the divine is beyond the material realm, while empirical science is within that realm.

The fact that every culture of which we know across all the

ages of history (or even prehistory) has had some expression of religion is a form of demonstration of the validity of the religious phenomenon. That has some aspects of circular reasoning, which will be clarified as we go on. This universality is also, however, a varied phenomenon. This variation is crucial, because it brings to light two further areas of investigation.

First, if the human response to the divine is so varied, one must determine what aspects of it are "true" or "real." Christians posit one eternal, intelligent, supernatural being who is the source and ground of all that is. The ancient Greek philosophers did the same but from a different perspective. Other religions claim a multiplicity of gods. Still others posit a non-personal force or energy. They cannot all be correct, because they are fundamentally opposed. Who got it right?

What Is Truth?

The second question raised by the variations within the universality is that of development over time. In ancient religions the gods controlled the rising and setting of the sun, the course of the seasons, and the fertility of the earth. As man has learned that these are natural phenomena and not the results of appeasing the gods in the proper manner, what had a religious explanation came to be understood outside the realm of religion—or at least requiring a different religious explanation.

The people who offer nonreligious (or antireligious) explanations of religion are often responding to these two fundamental concerns. They are not simply militant atheists (though they can be); they are asking valid questions that the phenomenon of religion has brought forward throughout history.

From the Christian perspective, we say that there is something about the human person that stirs one to ask ultimate questions: what is the meaning of life? What is happiness? Where did all the cosmos come from? What happens after death? These are questions all humans have burned to answer—they cannot help but ask them—and religion (or a philosophy that has distinctively religious overtones) has been the answer. Christians say that the human person has a "God-sized hole" (a desire or longing) that needs to be filled and can only be filled by God. People often try to address this longing with money, sex, power or fame; most have found these things lacking. That this longing exists is undeniable—perhaps not for everyone or at all times—but it is demonstrably evident in the course of human history.

Pontius Pilate asked Jesus, "Truth? What is truth?" (John 18:38). As a Roman official, he would have been educated and familiar with the various strains of philosophy current in his day. When he asks this question, he is well aware that many others have claimed to give testimony to the truth and that few of them were in even general agreement. In our day it is no different; we can (and must) ask the same question.

In response to the babel of voices pulling in every direction, one can feel overwhelmed and conclude that "truth"—if there is such a thing—is not knowable. The feeling is understandable; giving in to it is inexcusable. From Thales of Miletus (700 BC) to the present day, the greatest minds among us have always been convinced of two things: There is a truth and it can be known. The discovery of truth does indeed require hard work (Petronius was right), but it is well worth the effort (where he was wrong). The search for truth and meaning in life has been one of the animating principles, not only of religion and philosophy, but also of literature and drama.

Aristotle begins his *Metaphysics* with the simple sentence that: "All men by nature desire to know." In fact, as we will show later on, knowing anything at all requires building on certain truths already known—or at least accepted as true. By "nature," Aristotle was referring to the fact that "knowing" was the chief characteristic that distinguishes us from other members of the animal kingdom, This is another concept which must be unpacked more fully in our treatment of anthropology. At this stage we need only describe what form of an obstacle to conversion this notion presents.

When a person claims that truth is not knowable, it is rare that the person means it is not knowable per se. Most often, this attitude is more specific to the individual who gives voice to it. It is that "I" cannot know, not just any truth, but I cannot know the ultimate or foundational truths and cannot know them with such a degree of certainty as to allow conversion to faith to take place. All people know many truths—and many people think to be true many things that are not. Hence Will Rogers famous quip: "It isn't what we don't know that gives us trouble; it's what we know that ain't so."

This obstacle to conversion is understandable in that one has a justified trepidation to build one's life around an idea or a faith without knowing whether or not that idea or faith corresponds to reality. But it is also problematic in that the very nature of faith precludes absolute knowledge. Faith is, as Kierkegaard put it, "a leap." To reduce this obstacle, one must understand the nature of this leap (from where and into what) and the difference between surety and certitude.

Does Not Matter/Not Important

Perhaps all of this is true. But what about the obstacle that claims truth, as we have been discussing it here—truth that enables or undergirds faith—is simply unimportant? Or that it is too hard to discover and not worth the effort? Given the daily slog that constitutes many a life, who really can afford the leisure to ponder such questions? Is there any point to it all? Particularly given the degree with which so many who claim to have discovered "truth" do not agree with one another?

These are common and perhaps even valid questions. But they seem to fly in the face of claims made by some of the most esteemed thinkers in human history. Indeed, as we have already seen, they seem to strike at the very understanding of our human nature. If man is really the rational animal and desires above all else to know, then it would seem that it does matter, and it is important. The reason these questions are common is that they express a very real frustration that is part of being human. We really do desire truth and knowledge, but our experience is that they are often difficult to find. The resulting frustration over this problem (which is nothing more than simply being human) can spill out and take the form of these questions. It has also been the motive that has caused those great thinkers in human history to produce the writings we know as philosophy and theology.

Of course, most of us will not write great works of philosophy or theology; we simply are doing the best we can to get through life. Can it be true, then, that for most people truth does not matter or is not important? Not really; each of us has a worldview that is founded upon what we understand to be true or important. If this were not the case, we could scarcely get out of bed in the morning. Civilized society is built on the idea that there are truths and that they are important.

Think about driving your car. As you head to your destination, you naturally assume that the other drivers on the road will understand that the yellow stripe in the middle of the road has a meaning (this is my side and that is your side) and that the other drivers will understand and respect that meaning. You might say that this is a matter of the rules of the road, not about finding and knowing the truth. But we can have something like rules of the road only if there is such a thing as truth and it matters.

The alternative is often referred to as anarchy. Any rule, whether it is a formal law or simply a societal norm, relies on some common understanding of truth. Even our ability to communicate rests on a common understanding that ink marks on paper signify something we call letters; these can be formed into groups known as words, which also have a true meaning. Once you drill down far enough beneath the structure of everyday life, what you find is that truth and meaning are behind everything. Words, or anything else, have meaning only because there is a knowable truth about them. Truth and meaning are inseparable.

In fact, the simple truth about words and their meaning is terribly important. One of the main tactics of our adversary is to confuse language. This is famously illustrated by George Orwell's novel *1984*, but the insight was not original with him. Human history is full of examples where those in authority sought to change the perception of truth by giving new meanings to words people thought they knew well. This is done to mask the authorities' true intentions, which would be rejected if stated plainly. Whether it was Chairman Mao's great leap forward or Adolf Hitler's master race, the practice of changing language to mask intentions and gain acceptance has a long and tragic history. In our own day, the meaning of words like *gay*, *choice*, or *marriage* are being (or have been) redefined to gain acceptance for what had long been considered reprehensible. This is an aspect of the asymmetrical warfare in which the modern soldier is engaged.

This tactic is effective because it strikes at how the human intellect works. We seek meaning and truth and use language to communicate both. It is inescapable, because we are humans, and that is simply how we function. We function that way because we are made in the image and likeness of God, who is truth, and as that truth pours out into creation it becomes meaning. The glory of being human is that we are built to seek truth; the frustration is that it is sometimes hard to find.

Besides being an expression of frustration with being human, the idea that truth is either not knowable or unimportant really means that, in certain areas (almost always dealing with morality), people do not agree on what the truth is. When great (or common) minds disagree on what is and what ought to be, isn't it fair to say that there may be a truth "out there" and at the same time ask, how do we know it?

No, it is not fair! It would be fair only if what counted as truth was dependent on humans agreeing about it—or if at least a sufficient number of them agreed. In this view, the truth is arrived at by counting noses. Get enough people to agree—or get enough of the "right" people to agree—and one has arrived at truth. This approach to truth has given us the Holocaust, eugenics, slavery, and most of the other human horrors.

To be human is to exist in the realm of truth and therefore meaning. To consider it unimportant or someone else's responsibility is cowardly and—as history demonstrates—tragic.

The Concept of Sin

So perhaps there is truth. And perhaps it is vitally important for making determinations about how people ought to live. Even if this is true, is there really such a thing as sin? Sure there are bad decisions or bad laws, and people do bad things. And in order to call them "bad" there must be some standard against which these things can be measured. But is there really sin?

If my determination of the center of gravity is correct, then many of the obstacles noted above are really false obstacles. They are masks to hide the real obstacle, which is the demands of discipleship. Even if one were able to sufficiently reduce the other obstacles in this battlespace, until one deals with this one, scant progress toward the objective can be made. Some obstacles can be bypassed and reduced by follow-on forces. If this one is left intact, the enemy will be able to launch continued assaults from a position of strength that will make further movement impossible.

Sin adds three things to the categories of "bad" or "wrong": first, that there is Someone to whom we are accountable (God); second, that we can and should know better, because we have been given the tools to so know and do; third, there will be an accounting outside of time and history. Bad things happen to bad people, an eye for an eye, or "karma" are the effects of bad/wrong things within the created order. Sin is the idea that these things have a greater—indeed, an eternal—weight because they offend God.

Pope Pius XII lamented that the sin of the twentieth century was the loss of the sense of sin.[68] The idea has been echoed by many. Nearly every pope has said much the same thing. Why? Perhaps because so few are listening. This is one of those areas in which the Church itself has become an unwitting ally of the enemy. When the reality and ugliness of sin is replaced by words like *mistakes* or *harm* or even *injustice*, all three of the factors listed above are lost. We are simply fallible human beings in our temporal realm. We are that, but we are

---

68. 1946 radio address to the United States Catechetical Conference meeting in Boston.

far more. Our actions may be bad or wrong or unjust, but they are more. Failure to use the word *sin* and to understand it has consequences.

Does this mean that we ought to return to "fire and brimstone"? No; as Jesus pointed out to his disciples, that is the Father's job, not theirs (Luke 9:54–55). God sent fire to consume the inhabitants of Sodom and Gomorrah; Jesus sent his disciples to preach the good news and build the kingdom of God. But it is a kingdom of justice as well as of peace. God's peace is never without his justice. Unless we see sin and call it what it is, we are building, not his kingdom, but one more to our own liking.

Two Common Obstacles

There are two obstacles in our battlespace that can paralyze the unwary Christian warrior. Fortunately, they are also fairly easy to reduce. The novelist Flannery O'Connor once said, "You shall know the truth, and the truth shall make you odd." O'Connor was making a play on the scriptural quote, "You shall know the truth, and the truth shall make you free" (John 8:32). In the larger sense, she was pointing to another of the warnings from Jesus of Nazareth:

- If the world hates you, know that it has hated me before it hated you (John 15:18).

- And you will be hated of all for my name's sake (See Matthew 10:22a and Mark 13:13a).

Given that three of the four Gospel writers saw fit to include this warning, it might be an important one. Although our current age sees no shortage of those who truly do hate and even kill those who profess the gospel, that is not the most common form of this obstacle. More often, those who recoil at the call to conversion are fearful of two accusations: being called "judgmental" or "closed-minded."

"You're Judgmental!"

Fear of the first charge is an obstacle we can simply "cover by fire." Once it is understood properly, it loses its force. The obstacle will remain—people will still call you "judgmental"— but it will cease to be effective. This is because everyone is judgmental; it is just that some people admit it, while others don't. Being judgmental is unavoidable—every decision a person makes involves a judgment.

It is simply the necessary result of making a definition. By its very nature, the act of defining is an exercise in setting limits. A proper definition of a thing is constructed in such a manner that it describes the thing as it is. Depending on the thing being defined, it can be either broad or narrow. If it is a definition, it excludes those traits and characteristics that do not belong to the thing. In arriving at a definition, one must make choices as to what is included—and what is excluded— to arrive at accuracy.

If I define a tree as anything growing from soil and the nutrients therein, aided by sunlight and water, I fail to distinguish the tree from other types of plants. If I further define *tree* as something that has leaves and gray or brown bark, I have improperly excluded palm trees, fir trees, birch, and aspen. I have also excluded any tree grown under artificial light. Making accurate definitions is hard work. Certainly there are many times where a simple (though inaccurate) definition is sufficient for our communication to be properly understood. In fact, the word *tree* works just fine in most cases.

"Well," some might argue, "that is all well and good, but what about making moral judgments?" Our answer is that we make moral judgments all the time; if we did not, most of the criminal code would cease to exist. Murder and theft are crimes because we, as a society, have made a moral determination that they are wrong and cannot be tolerated. The question is not about whether we can make moral judgments about people's actions (or choices or perceptions of the good). It is a matter of deciding *who* makes the judgments and *by what standard*.

Is that standard the consent of the governed? This would seem to be the case for our criminal code. But is it really true? If enough people agree something is licit, then is it? Is truth really arrived at by counting noses? Can we trust that in a democratic society we would never arrive at the extreme?

Perhaps we can make moral judgments about matters widely recognized as criminal in most societies, but this is circular—the fact that it is against the law is already the result of a judgment. If you are accused of being judgmental, simply respond that everyone is and civilized society is built on rules that are judgments. This forces the one making the accusation to explain why this particular judgment with which he disagrees is wrong.

"You're Closed-Minded!"

This charge is made so often because it is so easy to make. Fortunately, it is equally easy to defeat. When one takes a firm position—again, usually on moral issues—one is often accused of being "closed-minded." What exactly does that phrase mean? When most people make such a charge, they intend to convey that they disagree with what the "closed-minded" person holds. The person making this charge really means that the other has accepted a certain point of view from a certain authority and is uninterested in exploring other points of view.

In order to make this accusation fairly, one must know that the person who is expressing a different view has not given the question careful study. This is almost never the case. A person may have arrived at a contrary position through years of careful consideration. It is rare indeed when one knows how much thought another has given to any particular decision. It may well be that his partner in dialogue has explored many different perspectives and come to a decision as to which one he will adopt. Rather than investigate the matter, it is much easier to accuse the other person of being closed-minded.

If you encounter this obstacle, the best approach is to simply challenge the one making the accusation. Ask him how he can possibly know what deliberation has led to your position. Since you can usually be certain that the accuser has no such knowledge, you have now thrown the burden on him to justify his own charge. As he will be unable to respond, the obstacle has been rendered ineffective.

With both these obstacles, note how the terrain is skewed largely toward questions of truth and knowledge. This is why apologetics is not wrong—it is absolutely necessary. But apologetics is always a supporting attack, never the main effort. What the devil hates, he attacks, and his fundamental attack against man is against his ability to know. We are the rational animal, so this attack strikes at what makes us what we *are*.

Sex: The Final Obstacle

Our final obstacle to overcome is the problem of the understanding of human sexuality. On July 17, 2013, *U.S. News & World Report* published an article with the eye-catching headline "Devout Catholics Have Better Sex." Given the caliber of the publication, it is not surprising that the headline and the article were (in order) misleading and old news. The article was based on a talk given by Patrick Fagan of the Family Research Council at the Center for the Advancement of Catholic Higher Education. The topic of the talk was on the effects of pornography on college campuses and drew on work done by Fagan and published in December 2009. His remarks on sexual satisfaction were quite brief and were drawn from an even older study conducted under the auspices of the University of Chicago and published as *Sex in America: A Definitive Survey*.[69] This work, the ultimate source of the headline, was published in 1994 using data from 1992.

The headline was accurate in the sense that the data do show that strongly religious married couples have sex more often than most other couples and are most happy with the sexual aspect of their life. I refrain from using the more common phrase "sex life," as it gives the sense that sex is a life of its own rather than an aspect of human life. This seems to be one of the key reasons behind the happiness of the religiously motivated married couples. They understand what sex is and what it is for. This seems to be a topic of confusion for many people today.

In Fagan's talk (and the paper from which it was drawn), he describes how the effects of pornography distort one's view of what sex is, how often it happens, and what activities take place. He shows how correct Edward Laumann (one of the authors of *Sex in America*) was when he stated that, for many people, there is a sense that they are missing out on what "everybody else" is doing. What the data show is that the reality of sex in America is not the fevered athletics depicted

---

69. John H. Gagnon, Edward O. Laumann, Robert T. Michael, and Gina Kolata, *Sex in America: A Definitive Survey* (Little, Brown & Company, 1994)

in most of our popular media. Rather, the norm is a more sedate practice of expressing love through physical intimacy. In a nutshell, sex is what the Church has said it was all along.

The prevailing perception, however, is that everyone else is having the sex described or depicted in the popular culture, and if our own practices are not the same, then we're deprived. We cannot be happy unless we're acting like the characters in *Fifty Shades of Grey*. Any attempt to shatter that illusion is met with hostility and denouncement. It is reminiscent of a line from the song "The Grand Illusion" by the seventies rock band Styx: "They'll show you photographs of how your life should be, but they're just someone else's fantasies."

As a society writ large, we are not (yet?) seeing human sexuality as Pope St. John Paul II did in *Love and Responsibility* (written while he was archbishop of Kraków) or in his Theology of the Body. But those who find the most satisfaction are closer to that ideal than they are to the depictions given us by the popular culture. What the data from the above-mentioned studies show is that the true practice of human sexuality is something quite different than what we are being sold.

This is the reason why the people most happy with the sexual aspect of their lives are devoutly religious married couples. They have seen through the distortions and have embraced the Christian teaching of chastity as the integration of one's sexuality into one's life in a manner fitting for their state in life (married, single, or vowed religious).

The one exception to this rule about the "sexual revolution" as a triumph of marketing is artificial contraception. Depending on which surveys one consults, more than 75 percent of Catholics and 90 percent of Protestants are using (or have used) some form of artificial means to regulate or avoid pregnancy. There are volumes of information on this topic, and this is not the venue to rehash all of it. It is certainly an obstacle for many people, but not one so formidable as it might seem, for it too is built on a lie (or rather two lies).

The first lie is that the ability to control or avoid pregnancy is necessary in a world that is overpopulated. Leaving aside Rev. Thomas Malthus, this has been an accepted premise since the publication of Paul Ehrlich's *The Population Bomb* in 1968. Like Malthus, his analysis was flawed, and his dire predictions have proven false. Yet almost every undergraduate I teach is convinced the world is on the brink of disaster due to overpopulation. Artificial methods of birth control are the answer to an artificial crisis.

The second lie is that the Pill (in particular) would liberate women from their own fertility. This lie is a bit more nuanced. Certainly the widespread acceptance of the birth control pill (or other means/devices) is among the factors that have allowed women to enter the workforce in numbers never before seen. Far more important was the long effort to gain women the vote and a proper education. The Pill came to the game in the bottom of the ninth inning but wanted the credit for all that had taken place before.

But there have been other effects not as salutary. As Pope Paul VI noted, among the consequences of artificial contraception would be

> marital infidelity and a general lowering of moral standards. Not much experience is needed to be fully aware of human weakness and to understand that human beings—and especially the young, who are so exposed to temptation—need incentives to keep the moral law, and it is an evil thing to make it easy for them to break that law. Another effect that gives cause for alarm is that a man who grows accustomed to the use of contraceptive methods may forget the reverence due to a woman, and, disregarding her

physical and emotional equilibrium, reduce her to being a mere instrument for the satisfaction of his own desires, no longer considering her as his partner whom he should surround with care and affection (*Humanae Vitae* 17).

It is no coincidence that the mainstreaming of pornography, the rise in infidelity, and the legalization of abortion have followed in the wake of the advent of artificial birth control. It is not the sole factor, but it is certainly a major contributor. Because it decoupled sex from the possibility of procreation, artificial birth control has fundamentally changed how people understand and approach human sexuality.

This is difficult to talk about with others. Most attempts at discussion of human sexuality evoke one of two responses. The first is a repetition of the mantras of the popular culture: people—especially young people—are going to do it anyway; you can't stop raging hormones; you have to live in the real world, not in some fantasy—the list goes on. My favorite is the last one, as it is an absolute inversion of reality.

Despite what the covers of women's magazines, Hollywood, and the porn industry try to sell us, every credible study shows that fevered gymnastics and constant availability are not the norm—or even close to it. It would seem that the marketing has become what everyone accepts as the norm, although they themselves are not living that way.

The second response one encounters (once it is established that one is speaking from a religious perspective) is: "You Catholics [or simply Christians] think sex is dirty, and people should do it only to have kids. It's all Puritan nonsense." There is some humor in this type of response. Given the size of most Puritan families, they were enjoying sex on a fairly regular basis. I am aware of no credible evidence that they found it distasteful.

What the Church Really Says

Humor aside, another problem is that everybody knows how the Church views sex—except few really *do* know. Instead, everyone knows what the popular culture tells them about how the Church views sex.

As you may have gathered by now, breaching this obstacle is not a matter of engaging it head-on and destroying it. The key for the spiritual warrior is to defeat the obstacle within yourself. Once you have accomplished that, the popular perception loses any force it once had. I am willing to bet that many men who are otherwise receptive to the message of this book are wavering before this obstacle. Worse yet, they may see sexuality in the way that young Augustine did: "God, grant me chastity . . . but not yet." Finally, there are those who would be warriors who do see the Church itself as the obstacle.

If you fall into either of these two latter categories, stop reading this book. If your vision of human sexuality is shaped by our popular culture, and you feel you cannot or should not change, you need remedial training. The front lines are no place for you. For those who are willing or even intrigued, read on.

Much of what the Church teaches about human sexuality is based on natural law. Merely observing human nature shows that sex is primarily about making babies. In the rest of the animal kingdom, sex is *only* about making babies. Since humans are members of that biological kingdom, sex is about making babies for us also. Of course, we are members of a supernatural kingdom as well, so there is more to the story. But there is also more to the story from a simple natural law perspective.

One of the key differences between us and lower-order

animals is our ability to experience pleasure in sexual activity. Most other members of the animal kingdom (Bonobos aside) seem to need physical stimuli to remind them it is time to mate. For most of them it is an instinct triggered at particular times, by specific physical or sensate changes. We can derive pleasure from sexual activity and can desire it without the need for specific stimuli. We are designed in such a manner that sex is different for us. Since God is our designer, it follows that he wanted sex to be about more than making babies.

Think of sex as analogous to eating. The primary end or goal of nutrition is health of the body. This we have in common with other animals. Like them, we can recognize which foods serve this end and which do not. Unlike other animals, we have been given an ability to discriminate tastes and to take pleasure in them. Certainly the koala "likes" eucalyptus leaves, but in an entirely different manner than a human can enjoy a steak (or chocolate, if you prefer). We have a primary need of nutrition for health of the body, but we are also designed to eat things simply because they taste good. Given that God designed us this way, the secondary good (taste) is not bad. This secondary good can become bad only by being disordered. If my desire (taste) for deep-fried Twinkies becomes more important than my need for healthy food, I will suffer.

In a similar manner, having sex because it is pleasurable is not bad. In fact, having sexual relations with one's spouse, at a time when one is reasonably certain it will not result in a pregnancy, is a good. But, like a diet of only deep-fried Twinkies, sex only for pleasure, and purposely excluding the possibility of pregnancy, is disordered. God gave us the ability to enjoy the physical aspects of sex, so it is okay to enjoy them. It is clear that God gave this ability to spur us to fulfill the command to be fruitful and multiply (Genesis 1:22, 1:28,

8:17, 9:1, 9:7, 35:11; Jeremiah 23:3; Ezekiel 36:11—the repetition may indicate the importance of the command).

Sex is pleasurable because God loves people and wants more of them. Only when the secondary good of pleasure eclipses the primary good of procreation is there a problem.

Remaining at the level of natural law and our difference from lower-order animals, we can also gain an appreciation for another dimension of sex. Humans are capable of abstract thought (hence imagination) and communication of meaning. We bring these attributes to any fully human understanding of sex. Humans can imbue actions with meaning and significance. We can, and should, understand that sex between human beings is about more than the pleasurable and procreative aspects. As a human act, it includes the intellectual abilities that are part of what it means to be human.

This aspect of sexuality is precisely what has been used to distort our understanding of sex. The "barbarians in Brooks Bothers suits"[70] have set in the imagination a false sense of what "everybody else is doing" to fire a desire for this missing "good," which promises ultimate pleasure. They have played us as a one would play a fiddle.

When we step beyond the natural law, we see how these human characteristics are to be properly used. Human sex is meant to be a physical expression of love. Husband and wife communicate their love and commitment to each other through the physical act of intercourse. In his Theology of the Body. Pope St. John Paul II showed that the only fully human way of engaging in sexual activity as God intended it was to be both life-giving (procreative) and love-giving.

The Church does not teach that sex is "dirty" or shameful

---

70. Fr. John Courtney Murray's characterization of advertising executives in the introduction to his *The Civilization of the Pluralist Society*.

or only for procreation. It teaches that it is beautiful—even glorious—and very much a part of God's plan. He commands humans to be fruitful and multiply and makes it extremely pleasurable to carry out this command. The enemy has infiltrated this aspect of humanity and perverted it.

Humans are made in the image and likeness of God. God is a communion of love between three divine Persons, where (according to St. Augustine) the love of two of those Persons brings forth the third one. If this is the case, then the most perfect human image of God is a man and a woman in the process of bringing about the existence of another person. Sexual intercourse is pleasurable by God's design: a means of fulfilling divine commands, a cooperation with God in continuing the species, and a most excellent human image of his divine image. This what the Church actually teaches about sex.

Of course, far more could be said about this great obstacle. I encourage all spiritual warriors to further discover this hidden treasure of the Church. Finding the true beauty of human sexuality is not just for those who would otherwise be unfit for service. It is necessary for happiness, conversion, and evangelization. That aspect presented here is sufficient to defeat the obstacle.

Our battlespace is littered with obstacles. The enemy has planned carefully and well. But those obstacles that can seem so imposing are generally only as strong as we allow them to be. They gain most of their effectiveness from our own weakness, fear, or lack of knowledge. To defeat them often requires a simple change in perspective or attitude. In some cases it requires a renewal of the mind so that the warrior is not conformed to this age (see Rom. 12:2). Only in a few cases will they require a deeper conversion of heart. But all of these things are necessary steps in the training of the spiritual warrior.

SUPPORTING ATTACK

The human condition; considered in its broadest perspective, has three primary problems:

- We are human but aspire to be something more.

- We are mortal but rebel against our end.

- We are ordered toward—or desirous of—the good and at the same time capable of great evil.

One could make the argument that most of the world's great literature and drama revolves around one or all of these three problems.

Destined for Glory

The first problem, at least on the surface, is based on how different we are from other members of the animal kingdom. We are quantitatively and qualitatively different, and there seems to be no upper limit to the capabilities of our species. This naturally leads man to the idea that he is destined for glory. And so he is. The problem laid bare by human history is that every time man acts on this desire to be superman, tragedy follows.

The tragedy is a fruit of our misunderstanding—not our misunderstanding that we are more than simply human but our misunderstanding of how to respond to that desire. We have indeed been made little less than a god (see Psalm 8), and we do desire more. It is a natural desire, and therefore it must have an object that will satisfy it. The proper manner of responding to that desire is not by activity but by receptivity.

It is not by grasping for power, wealth, fame, or glory; Aristotle saw that these were not adequate even to ensure happiness. We satisfy our desire to be "like God" not in our human way but by allowing ourselves to be transformed in his way.

If every human attempt to achieve divine (or semi-divine, i.e., superman) status has been met with failure, and often tragedy. So why do we continue to try it our way? If the definition of insanity is doing the same thing and expecting different results, then striving for an elevated status is insanity. We are indeed made little less than a god. We are also meant to one day participate in the very life of the Father, Son, and Holy Spirit. We are supposed to be more God-like than even the wildest dreams of history's idealists. We simply need to receive the graces necessary and allow the transformation to take place. The forbidden fruit and tower of Babel were warnings about this greedy grasping after divinity. Sanity is to heed the lesson.

The Reality Is Immortality

The second problem concerns death. The human person, like any other organism, will die. This is natural. It has also been a constant theme of human reflection: why must it be so? There seems to be something in the human spirit that rebels against the idea of death. We find death to be repugnant at a level most of us find difficult to describe. What can account for this nearly universal reaction to the simple fact of our mortality?

The zebra on the African veldt may experience something we would recognize as terror when the lion springs from cover. But the zebra, absent the lion, does not ponder death, nor its inevitability. Is it only our greater intellectual capacity that accounts for the human response? I would argue it is because we are truly designed for unending life.

To remain for the moment with our analogy from the rest of the animal kingdom, we see what looks like mourning behavior among certain species when a member of the group has been killed. Is this because they sense a loss? Feel the absence that the loved one used to fill? More important, is this all there is to our own sadness at the death of a loved one?

I will not comment on the degree to which the behavior in lower-order animals is evidence of an intellectual or emotional process similar to what humans experience. This is far from my area of expertise. From what I have read, there seems to be a certain degree of anthropomorphism in claims being made for how the zebra or the monkey "feels" or "thinks." Without being able to plumb the depths of the animal psyche, I doubt that we can make many certain judgments. The fact that we cannot even fully understand our own thoughts, emotions, and processes should be enough to make one doubt that we accurately determine what is going on in other animals.

Even if there are parallels between us and other animals in response to death, I think it is fair to say that there is a great distance—both quantitative and qualitative—between the human response to the fact of inevitable death and those observed in lower species.

We rebel against the idea of an end to ourselves and to our loved ones because in the beginning it was not so. The story of Adam and Eve is meant to show us what we were intended for and the magnitude of what we lost due to sin. The human person really is intended to be an existence without end, and our communion with those we love is meant to be everlasting.

If the wages of sin is death (see Romans 6:23), it follows that, without sin, there would not have been death. Because Adam was an animal organism, he was capable of dying. If a large rock had fallen on his head, he would have died. But absent some misfortune, old age would not have spelled his doom. In theological jargon, this is referred to as immortality and was a preternatural gift super-added to human nature.

Though we have been deformed by sin, we still retain some memory of this gift. We rebel against death even though it seems senseless to do so. But God is merciful and keeps his promises. The preternatural gift of immortality has been changed into a blessing and a curse. The immortality remains, but now it carries with it a reward or a punishment. When our life on Earth is over, the rest of eternity will be spent somewhere.[71] We hope that most of us will spend the rest of eternity in heaven, with a preliminary stop in purgatory. Actually, a true Christian hope would replace "most" with "all" and eliminate the stop in purgatory; but I'm enough of a realist (or lousy enough of a Christian) to hope for the lesser good. The other option is to spend the rest of eternity in hell.

The fact that these topics are rarely preached on Sundays does not mean they are any less real. In fact, our immortality and the options it entails are not just real, they are more real than the passing things of this life on which we tend to focus. Sanity is being in touch with reality. Reality is immortality.

Good and Evil

The third problem, that of good and evil, is unique to the human species. Every major world religion has made some attempt to explain what went wrong with the human person. By "what went wrong" I refer to the simple observation that most people are oriented toward the good. At the same time, those same people are capable of committing evil. So

---

71. Not a physical or spatial "somewhere" but a state of being our language is inadequate to explain.

the solution to this third problem is to uncover what accounts for this duality.

One of the things that make this problem so challenging is that there are a variety of ways of describing the "good." Even if people cannot agree on what the "good" is, there is at least general agreement that the good is what most people desire. Those who desire evil are, and have always been, considered at least odd, if not criminal or insane. An example I use with my students is that no one desires to strangle puppies. More precisely, those who do desire to strangle puppies are considered to have some sort of pathology that accounts for this desire. Use whatever analogy or example you would prefer, but there are certain types of desires that all cultures and all peoples have found to be outside those that constitute normal human behavior. There is a natural moral law. Even if people today would argue what it consists of, we are not yet (in any meaningful sense) at the point where all morality is seen as mere social construct. There are those who make this argument, but they have little influence outside of particular pockets of academia. The real problem lies in defining what constitutes the good, or the natural moral law.

A brief digression is necessary at this point to clarify some of my terminology. In academic circles today, the discussion of being human is fraught with controversy. Some object to any attempt to describe things as either normal or abnormal. "Normal" is considered entirely a social construct.[72] Even the idea that there is something that can be called "human nature" is rejected out of hand.[73]

I follow the way of Aristotle, who believed that, when con-

---

72. "The Range of Normal in Human Behavior," *Psychosomatics,* vol. 18, no. 4; Oct. 1977, p. 55.
73. See Steven Pinker's *The Blank Slate: The Modern Denial of Human Nature.*

sidering the human person, one should use as the benchmark
not the most base, or even the most common, but the highest
example.[74] Of course, as Aristotle noted, the argument over
the good and human nature has been going on for quite some
time. It continues to the present day; but at some point one
needs to decide where one stands in regard to these fundamental principles. It is far beyond the scope of this work to
settle the matter. My intention in this digression is merely to
point out on what side of the ledger I fall and what my assumptions are about the good and human nature.

Although this is not the place to settle these issues, the
simple point can be made that, in order for human society
to function, there must be bottom-line moral norms that
must not be crossed. In order for humans to flourish (another
of Aristotle's ideas, though he called it *eudaimonia*), a higher
moral code is necessary. To live as God intends, the fullness
of the moral laws as revealed by Christ and his Church is
intended. People of good will and sound mind can (and will)
argue over the specifics, but it is a matter simply of sanity to
recognize that there is need of a moral law. It serves both to
stand as a bulwark against the baser urges of our nature and a
guarantor of our better ones.

Thus far, belief as the only sane manner of living has focused on three particular problems of human existence. This
is trying to make a point by showing that, at a bare minimum,
these points validate the argument. I am convinced we can do
better than that. In fact, libraries are full of the works of philosophers and theologians who make the case for adherence
to Christianity as the only sane way for a person to live. But a
supporting attack is never to be mistaken for the main effort.
If a commander expends too much of his time and energy

74. Aristotle, *Ethics*, book I, ch. 8.

making his supporting attack; the main attack suffers. I will not make that error here.

The problems we face—those particular to our day and community as well as those endemic to humanity—have an answer. Indeed, some of them have more than one good answer. The answers revealed by God have stood the test of time and produced saints beyond counting and happiness in the face of misery for millions.

Denial, either of the problems or their solutions, may be popular or win elections, but denial is not sanity. Denial is living in the world we wish we had rather than the one we have. It is wishing that people are like we hope they would be, not as they are. Denial is popular, but it has deadly consequences. Facing the real human problems in the real world is unpleasant but necessary. It is necessary because it is real and living in the "real" is sanity.

4

ADMINISTRATION
AND LOGISTICS

THE ADMINISTRATION AND LOGISTICS PARAGRAPH
CONTAINS ALL THE DETAILED ADMINISTRATIVE
INFORMATION THAT DOES NOT FIT ELSEWHERE.

In my experience as a Marine, this was the part of the order that the operations officer hated to write. As I gained more experience, I saw that the best tactical plan in the world was either worthless or a potential disaster until these "administrative" details were worked out. Having a grand scheme of maneuver to crush the enemy is great; not having sufficient fuel or ammunition to execute it is not.

CATEGORIZING THE ESSENTIALS

One simple way of organizing this part of the order and ensuring nothing essential is left out is to focus on four major categories:

- Beans: anything that is a personal consumable—food and water, for example

- Bullets: all types of munitions and pyrotechnics that are needed

- Band-Aids: all aspects of medical care, from the corpsman's kit bag to medevac and field hospitals

- Bad guys: what one is to do with prisoners of war, wounded enemy combatants, and civilian refugees

A complex but essential section of the order was easy to remember using the beans, bullets, Band-Aids, and bad guys approach, so I will use the same one here. I will also limit the number of topics I include in each area. Any number of things could be included, but I will focus on a few essentials. As we will see, many of these "administrative" matters also constitute our continual training. Warriors train, even in the midst of combat operations. In spiritual combat, training is not just for keeping our skills sharp; it is our primary means of engaging the enemy on the ground of our choosing (not his). For this reason (and since you have made it this far into the book), I will provide some "suggestions" for your training.

BEANS: PRAYER AND THE EUCHARIST

The two sacraments that ought to be received on a regular basis (confession and Communion) have a parallel in the military. Communion is analogous to both physical nourishment and to continuing training in which one engages within his particular specialty. The infantryman who stops continually practicing his skills in land navigation or patrolling will be a failure—and failure as an infantryman can lead to death. The Christian who either does not receive his Lord in the Eucharist or receives him while not recognizing his body, blood, soul, and divinity is similarly doomed.

For as often as you eat this bread, and drink the cup, you proclaim the Lord's death till he comes. Whoever, therefore, eats the bread or drinks the cup of the Lord in an unworthy manner, will be guilty of profaning the body and the blood of the Lord. Let a man examine himself, and so eat of the bread, and drink of the cup. For anyone who eats and drinks without discerning the body eats and drinks judgment upon himself. That is why many of you are weak and ill, and some have died (1 Cor. 11:26-30).

The sacrament of confession, properly understood, ought to be received nearly as often as one receives the Eucharist. Certainly, if one must be in the state of grace to worthily approach the Eucharist (and that means not conscious of any mortal sin), then most people should be frequenting the confessional much more than they do. We will look at this sacrament more closely under "Band-Aids." For now, we return to Communion and prayer as our "beans."

Any good warrior wants to ensure he has a firm grasp on his commander's intent. This is particularly important in "mission-type" orders. You will recall that this type of an order was used when a linear explanation of tactics could not be used, since it was not clear what the enemy was likely to do or where/when he would be encountered. This is the situation in spiritual combat. The enemy may be encountered in various ways and at any time or location. Understanding our commander's intent, mission, and vision is essential.

Interiorizing Our Orders

In spiritual combat, we have the means of truly interiorizing our commander. In the Eucharist, we receive the body, blood, soul, and divinity of Christ. In doing so, we have the greatest

possible means by which to enter into his mission. Cardinal
Balthasar understood Jesus of Nazareth as the ultimate "theological person." This phrase meant a person who so identified
with his mission that he became that mission—it filled every
thought and action and defined who he was. Certainly, Christ
is our exemplar in this area. He told his disciples, "I have food
to eat that you do not know of" (John 4:32). That "food" was
to do his Father's will (John 4:34).

After the Last Supper, we too have this food. By eating his
flesh and drinking his blood (see John 6:27ff) we have life and
mission imparted to us. There is simply no greater gift than to
receive him into our own bodies. There can be no option but
failure should we neglect to use this gift. A warrior who is not
properly nourished and hydrated cannot be successful in the
ardors of combat. The spiritual warrior who does not receive
the Eucharist is unfit for battle.

But the sacraments are not magic. They are efficacious,
meaning that they are capable in themselves of achieving
what they are meant to achieve. In order for them to have
their intended effect, we need two things: the proper disposition and active cooperation with the graces received. In the
case of the Eucharist, the proper disposition includes freedom
from sin and the attachment to sin—hence the necessity of
confession. Active participation with grace is found in prayer.
We can receive him into our bodies in a physical manner, but
until he is received into our soul and our mind, we have not
activated those graces.

Prayer: What God Does for Us

Prayer is essential. It allows us to develop that proper disposition and is the means by which the graces received become active in us. St. Paul told the Christians at Rome to "be

enlightened by the renewal of your minds" (Rom. 12:1-2). Prayer is the manner in which one uses the physical body of Christ to bring about the renewal of the mind so that one's entire self becomes dedicated to the mission of Christ. He was entirely defined by accomplishing his mission. If we want to be similarly focused on our own mission, we must become like him. The twin tools of prayer and Eucharist are how we are fed and train for spiritual combat.

So what kind of prayer is necessary? Simply put: any and all, because prayer is far more about what God does in us than what we do. The Holy Spirit is able to use any form of prayer and turn it to our advantage. Earlier in his letter to Rome, St. Paul noted that we really do not know how to pray but that the Holy Spirit will make up for our deficit (Rom. 8:26-28). So, in reality, any and all forms or prayer can work. But there are three forms of prayer that the experience of the Church has brought to prominence.

The first of these is the liturgy. The word *liturgy* means "public work." It is the public form of the "work" of praising and worshipping God. I will make only brief comments on this foremost form of prayer, since I assume most readers are participating—both inwardly and outwardly—at Mass. Note that the inward participation precedes the outward. If one is not interiorly offering himself as a sacrifice (to God, Church, and family) while Christ is being offered in sacrifice on the altar, no amount of outward participation has its true meaning or effect.

The liturgical prayer of the Church is not limited to the holy sacrifice of the Mass. Each member of the Christian faithful is called and encouraged to pray the Divine Office. If you intend to be a knight in Christ's army, pray at least some parts of the Divine Office. Also known as the Liturgy of the Hours, this is an ancient and powerful way to continue your training. It is mandatory for the ordained members of the army, but it is also highly recommended for all the baptized. Learn it, pray it, and, if your parish does not sponsor it already, lead it.

Efficacious Scripture Reading

The second ancient and important form of prayer is reading Scripture. This can be any daily reading from the Bible, "daily" being the operative word. Of course, if you are praying the Liturgy of the Hours or participating in daily Mass, you are already reading/hearing Scripture. The more advanced training one still needs is something called *lectio divina*. This refers to the habit of daily reading of Scripture in a particular manner. There are many ways to accomplish this form of prayer, and the "right" one is the one that works for the individual. A suggestion from those members of God's army we call saints is this:

- Pick a particular passage from one of the four Gospels; perhaps the one used for Mass that day.

- Read it slowly and carefully, repeatedly.

- Picture yourself in the scene as it unfolds. Think about what it would be like to be there. What does it sound like, look like, or even smell like? What time of day is it, and where are you standing? What role are you playing, participant or spectator?

- As you do all of this, ask the Holy Spirit to open your mind to the particular message he wants you to find in this particular reading at this particular moment.

We do this not to become "experts" in anything other than the habit of prayer—particularly prayer as the Church has discovered it to be most helpful. Helpful in what? In becoming attuned to the same Spirit who inspired the apostles and Scripture. Some might think that a lay person praying the Divine Office is "putting on airs," since this is a practice that has been the province of clergy and religious for centuries. In fact, it is the opposite: it is an exercise in humility. It is a manner of saying (with St. Paul) that we do not know how to pray as we should.

A good soldier follows orders even when he does not fully understand them. He recognizes that his commander has good reason for the orders, and, even if he does not have the whole picture, he obeys. So pray the office as an exercise of humility and obedience. What you will find is that becoming attuned to the Holy Spirit is a continually unfolding gift. That same Spirit we received at baptism is alive in Scripture (and the Divine Office is almost entirely Scripture). That same Spirit is also the promised and unfailing guide of the Church (see John's account of the Last Supper; chapters 13-17). Here we see Jesus telling his disciples about the role the Holy Spirit would play in his Church and in their lives.

Place yourself into that scene and imagine those words, prayers, and promises being directed to you personally. They are not static words spoken to other people in the distant past. They truly are words spoken to every Christian at every moment in time. The encounter with Christ is waiting in the Gospels. It is discovered through the contemplative reading of Scripture (the *lectio divina*) and continued in the public prayer of the Church. Become humble or "docile to the Spirit" and follow him into prayer. Let the Spirit become the one who prays within you.

This is the humility and obedience the spiritual warrior

must develop. It is also something that goes against the grain for many people today. The demands of discipleship begin with interior humility and obedience, because that was what Jesus lived during his time on Earth. He was humble enough to take on the likeness of a slave (Philem. 2:5ff). In the Incarnation, the second person of the Trinity sets aside some aspects of his divinity so that he can become fully human. He is then obedient to his Father as the Holy Spirit sets the Father's will before him at each moment. Our humility and obedience must follow the pattern he established. The modern knight has to empty himself and become obedient to the Father's will as made known to him through the Spirit, because this is the pattern set by Christ—the pattern of redemption.

BULLETS: LOVE AND KNOWLEDGE

In our examination of the human person, we saw that the two major faculties (or operations) of the soul are intellect and will. If these are primarily what make us human, it will come as no surprise that we need ammunition for each. If one's encounter with Christ is an encounter between two persons, then the whole human person must be engaged by the whole divine person. The person who enters spiritual combat must have resources (for himself and others) that support both the heart and the head, the will and the intellect.

The heart (which is the will) is moved by a desire that grows into love. The ultimate object of the desire and love is God. But how that desire is aroused and how one falls in love will be different for different people. In order to be effective in our training and actions as spiritual warriors, we have to understand how love works. Poets have long recognized that love is a many-splendored thing. It seems the more we speak about mere human love, the more remains to be said. If this is the case for love between two human beings, how much more so it must be for love between a human and God.

Love of God

For some, love of God comes naturally. We see the depiction of Jesus in the Gospels and love the One we see there. As in human love, there is often one particular thing that catches the eye of the heart. It may be the wise teacher, the caring humanitarian, the healer of those who are sick, or even the stern judge who rebukes the religious leaders of his day. We see all of these "faces" of Christ in the Gospels. Regardless of which face we find initially attractive, we need to learn to love all of them.

When we truly love another human being, the more we learn about that person, the more we grow to love the entire person. One aspect of that person may have initially attracted us, but we cannot get enough. Even when we discover something that we might not find so lovable in others, it becomes lovable when we see it in our beloved (even if it takes a while to develop that love). If human love works this way, why should we expect our love for God to be any different?

Certainly, it is different when we consider God's love for us; but we can love only as humans love, because that is what we are. So we fall in love with Christ one step at a time, and a mature love embraces all that we find in the man Jesus of Nazareth. We don't pick and choose what we like or dislike; we say with St. Thérèse of Lisieux, "I choose all."

Love of Self

For others, either the warrior or the one the warrior seeks to evangelize, the first step is not love of God but love of self.

Too much love of self can be an obstacle. As we have seen, it can be what causes a person to shy away from the demands of discipleship. But what about the person who lacks adequate self-love? In our fallen world, many people see themselves as unworthy of love. Because they cannot love themselves, they think they are unlovable by others. Certainly, they are not worthy of God's love.

The remedy here is that they are correct: they are not worthy of God's love. Neither is anyone else. No one outside the Trinity is worthy to draw the admiration of God. Rather, it is the fact that one is loved by God that imparts worth to the human person. To see human worth as measured by the esteem of other humans is laughable. The surpassing worth of all human beings is that God loves them enough to die for them. Those who see themselves as unlovable have, perhaps, simply never been loved by another human being. They certainly do not understand that such a love is often fickle and always transitory. The truth of each person is based on the fact that he or she is loved by God himself. This is an indication that our love for others should follow suit.

Love of Others

Finally, we turn to love of others. We may begin with love of God, and through it learn to love ourselves, because he loved us first. But a full flowering of Christian love always spills out into love of others. This happens for two reasons. The first is that the very nature of love (human or divine) is that it always seeks an object. Love is always directed toward a beloved; that is simply what love is. The second reason is that, if we truly love God, we will necessarily love all that he loves—and that means everybody.

Learning to love God and ourselves is part of basic training.

Advanced training includes learning to love those we seek to evangelize. One of the greatest evangelists of the early Church was St. Paul. He wrote that without love, he was useless (see 1 Cor. 13). Love desires the good of the beloved. In evangelization, it is the desire that the person we seek to evangelize come to know the good that we have found in faith in Christ.

There are two extremes that must be balanced in this love we have for others. Virtue is always the mid-point between two vices. As we have seen, balance is necessary. In evangelization the vices are: 1) trying to force love of God down someone's throat, and 2) love that fails to rebuke. When Paul wrote that love is patient and kind (1 Cor. 13:4), he did not mean it was all sunshine and butterflies. Inspired by God, Paul could be forceful with those he loved. (See his letters to the Galatians or the Corinthians.)

Love as evangelization has traditionally been called a "zeal for souls." The problem with this description lies in the word "zeal." That zeal can work mistakenly toward either end of the spectrum. We can be so anxious that others see the beauty of God's love that we can be overbearing—or can be interpreted that way, which is the same thing. In these cases love needs to be gentle and patient. Zeal can also cause us to so desire conversion and repentance that we neglect repentance in favor of conversion. In this case, love needs to follow the pattern of 1 Corinthians 5:2-5:

And you are arrogant! Ought you not rather to mourn? Let him who has done this be removed from among you. For though absent in body I am present in spirit, and as if present, I have already pronounced judgment in the name of the Lord Jesus on the man who has done such a thing. When you are assembled, and my spirit is present, with the power of our Lord Jesus, you are to deliver this man to

Satan for the destruction of the flesh that his spirit may be saved in the day of the Lord Jesus.

Nothing can cause mission failure more quickly than failing to find the proper balance in love for others. Zeal for souls is a good thing, but too much of a good thing can be bad. There is a time for rescuing a lost sheep and a time for overturning tables. The well-trained warrior recognizes the situation and responds with the appropriate action.

Love of Enemies

Finally, we need to love even our enemies (see Matt. 5:44, Luke 6:27). Those who are arrayed against us in spiritual combat are our enemy. But the same love that motivates our encounter with those we seek to evangelize must motivate our contact with the enemy—because in most cases, they are the same people. The only enemies we are allowed not to love are Satan and his demons. Everyone else gets love in proper form and measure.

This can happen only after we have learned to see love as it truly is. Human love is most authentic when it mirrors the way God loves. God loves even those who act contrary to his will. He shows his love for them by chastisement and correction. We ought to love our enemies in the same manner. The ultimate goal is for them to arrive at conversion of heart, because in that way you have won your brother (see Matt. 18:15). In fact, the eighteenth chapter of St. Matthew's Gospel is a guidebook for love in tough situations: verses 8-9 tell us what self-love looks like when dealing with temptations to sin, and verses 12-17 address the love one ought to show toward enemies in order to win them back for Christ. Verses 21-22 summarize the guide to love. St. Matthew closes this lesson in love with a parable that explicitly uses God's love as the measure.

Note that this treatise on love is not all sunshine and rainbows. Verse six pronounces sentence on those who corrupt children; verse seven is a lament over the fate of any who are the source of temptation to sin. When forced to choose between bodily health and spiritual sickness, we are to take drastic measures even with ourselves. This is tough love from the One who is love. Note also that St. Matthew points to the role and authority of the Church in verses 17-18. The first is particular to the case of the sinner who refuses to repent; the latter is a general rule for all. We do love our enemies and ourselves, but there may be pain involved.

Sources of Knowledge

Our most important type of ammunition is love that addresses itself to the human will. The second type of munition we need is knowledge. As with love, it is knowledge as training (for ourselves) and as a means of engaging others. Much of this book has been devoted to specific aspects of knowledge. Here I intend only to note the sources on which one can rely to gain this ammunition.

Because we cannot know in advance what the enemy will present us with, we cannot have a ready-made intellectual answer that will always work. Every time we make contact, the situation will be different. What the spiritual warrior needs to accomplish his mission-type order is the knowledge of where to look for the specific answers he needs to objections he might meet. Often, the intellectual objections with which we are faced are nothing more than a screen for the underlying fear of the demands of discipleship. It may really be fear at work more so than a question. But before we can deal with the fear (through love), we need to clear away the questions. It may also be that the questions are the only things holding back love that is otherwise ready to blossom. In either case, one must know where to turn.

The warrior could spend years studying and learning, and there is nothing wrong with that. It simply is not necessary. There are countless sources of "book learnin'," but if that is where our focus is, we have misunderstood the nature of the question. We need a deep immersion in prayer and love; the rest will follow.

But there are times when we do need to turn to trusted sources to answer specific objections. The first two sources (in order of importance) are the Bible and the *Catechism of the Catholic Church*. The third source is something the tradition calls the *sensus fidelium*, or what we may simply call a BS detector. Let's look briefly at each of these sources.

Sacred Scripture (aka the Bible)

Since we have already covered how Scripture and Tradition are the two sources of revelation (chapter 1), we can move to how Scripture was assembled. The individual books are inspired by God; the table of contents was determined by the Church. In the earliest days of Christianity, Scripture was what we now call the Old Testament. Many of the Church Fathers wrote treatises showing how Jesus of Nazareth was spoken of in the Hebrew holy scrolls. They wanted to show how he had been predicted by the prophets and had fulfilled those prophecies. Over time, the book(s) of the prophet Isaiah were given the nickname "the fifth Gospel," because so much of what he wrote about was accomplished by Jesus (and John the Baptist).

During the early centuries of the Christian era, many authors sought to capture the stories of Jesus and the Church he started. Eventually, the bishops recognized a need to draw up a list of those Christian writings that God had inspired. One early proposed list was drawn up by a wealthy merchant named Marcion. He presented his list to the Church at Rome, along with a sizable donation of money. Both his list and his money were rejected. He wanted the Old Testament to be cast aside so that Christians would be guided only by St. Luke's Gospel and ten of St. Paul's letters. The Church understood that these books alone did not capture all that was needed to preserve the "rule of faith."

As the centuries progressed, more of what we now know to be New Testament came to be widely understood as inspired by God. By about A.D. 250, although there was a fairly stable and widely accepted list, or canon, books were still included by some Christians or left out by others. Books such as the "Shepherd of Hermes," the "Prayer of Manasseh," and the "First Letter of Clement" were on the list or weren't, depending on whom you asked or where you looked. Eventually, the canon as we know it was drawn up at the Council of Carthage in 397.

An earlier council (at Orange, in 393) had settled the canon of the Old Testament. For centuries, the Jews had (at least) two dominant lists of Scripture. Scholars today refer to them as the Palestinian and Alexandrian canons. The latter (written in Greek for the majority of Jews who did not live in the Holy Land and spoke little or no Hebrew) was considerably longer than the former. The Old Testament canon used by Christians was the Alexandrian version, collected in what we know as the Septuagint. So (nearly) four centuries after the founding of Christianity, we had a Bible. It would not be significantly changed until the sixteenth century by Martin Luther—although his changes to the New Testament were short-lived.

More important than how we got the Bible is what we do with it and how we understand it. We have already addressed the role of Scripture in prayer, so only two points remain to be made. The first is that the same Holy Spirit who inspired the authors of the various books is the same one who guides the Church and the one we receive in the sacraments (particularly baptism and confirmation). Because he is divine and therefore perfect, the Holy Spirit does not suffer from multiple personality disorder. If ever there seems to be a discrepancy between the individual books—and at first glance there are some—the resolution can be found. More importantly, if there seems to be a contradiction between what the Holy Spirit says in Scripture and what he says via the Church; there is a need for a closer reading, because there can be no real difference. Most importantly, if what the Spirit speaks to you in your conscience differs from Scripture or Church teaching, you are wrong. The first step in resolving such a difficulty is humility. Until you admit that you might have an error in your thinking, you are not really ready to look for the answer.

The Holy Spirit speaks to us in the depth of our conscience, but he also speaks through Scripture. He is of one mind, and if a difficulty is encountered, either the individual or God must be in error; and it is safe to assume God is not wrong. So how does one resolve the problem (assuming the humility step has been taken)? Not surprisingly, prayer is the second step. In fact, before reading any Scripture, it is a good idea to begin with prayer. A traditional one goes something like this:

> Spirit of wisdom, enlighten me to understand what I am about to read, and help me put it into practice.

Assist my memory to retain what you desire should later be used in the interests of charity, and the work of my vocation.

Teach me to recognize in this reading an instrument of your grace, directing my soul to greater union with you, and through me, the souls of others with whom I share what you wish me to learn. Amen.

The *Catechism*

It has been said that the Council of Trent stole the idea of a catechism from Martin Luther. It would be more accurate to say that the title "catechism" was borrowed and applied to a very old idea. Beginning in the second century A.D., it was common for bishops to develop a basic set of teachings for new converts. These were the original catechisms and were often an elaboration of the Creed. Most people today are familiar with the Apostles Creed and the Nicene Creed, the latter of which is used in the Mass. Creeds were initially developed by each bishop as summaries of what it meant to be a Christian. They were used in the liturgy and as a guide for the instructions converts received from the deacons. After many centuries, some creeds came to be widely accepted across many dioceses. At Trent, the decision was made to have a single authoritative catechism for the entire Church (now referred to as the *Roman Catechism*).

Today's version of the *Catechism* was issued by Pope St. John Paul in 1992. He wrote that it is a "sure guide" to the essential teachings of the Church. When it was released, many theologians and religious educators sought to convince people it was not to be read by the "simple folk"; they should rely on the theological experts to distill it for them. This was largely because it dispelled many errors that were popular among those same theologians and religious educators. Fortunately, those warnings were ignored, and people bought the book in droves.

Because of this, many erroneous notions about Catholicism have been dispelled. But there are still pockets of resistance, particularly (but not exclusively) in the area of moral theology. Many of these errors are attractive, because they are presented as being merciful. They seek to blunt the sharp edges of discipleship. But lies, regardless of how they are presented, are never charitable. This is a problem as old as the Church herself. St. Irenaeus of Lyon wrote:

Error, indeed, is never set forth in its naked deformity, lest, being thus exposed, it should at once be detected. But it is craftily decked out in an attractive dress, so as, by its outward form, to make it appear to the inexperienced (ridiculous as the expression may seem) more true than the truth itself.[75]

The *Catechism* not only covers all things one might need to know, it does so in three different "layers." The simplest layer is found at the end of each section, where the essentials of a topic are presented "in brief." These sections are short, and each serves as a summary of the section that precedes it. Obviously, the second layer is those individual sections, each covering in all the necessary detail any particular topic. The third layer is the footnotes. If reading the text of the *Catechism* is not enough, there are thousands of footnotes directing the reader to even more detailed treatments of each topic. Naturally, the majority of these footnotes refer to the Bible. The collection of documents of the Second Vatican Council is the second-most-cited source, and the writings of other saints come in third.

75. Irenaeus, *Against the Heresies*, book 1, §2.

Between Sacred Scripture and the *Catechism*, most people will have all the wisdom they can stomach. The third part of our resources is the only missing piece.

The Sense of the Faithful *(Sensus Fidelium)*

I place this resource third, even though, in a sense, it comes before the other two. Properly speaking, the *sensus fidelium* (Latin for "sense of the faithful") refers to the unified awareness of truth in the Church. The members of the Body of Christ will always give their assent of mind and will to what the Church teaches. This is because the faithful, who have formed their conscience according to the mind of the Church, cannot fail to be united to it. The Holy Spirit does not suffer from multiple personality disorder. The Spirit speaks with the same voice (the same truth) in the scriptures, in the magisterium, and in the consciences of the faithful. In the sacraments, Catholics receive the gifts of the Holy Spirit, including wisdom and understanding to know and love the truth.

A side effect of this indwelling of the Holy Spirit, if actively nourished, is that "gut feeling" we have that something is true or false. This is first and foremost a gift: a good religious education and the habit of clear, logical thinking may make it more effective, but as long as we have received the Holy Spirit, we have this gift. When we nourish the gift by prayer, sacrament, and an active listening to the magisterium, we will be able to tell when something we hear or read doesn't sound right. We may not know exactly what is wrong or why it is wrong; but that interior alarm will go off. It is the Holy Spirit nudging us away from error and back to truth.

A good religious education is not just something one gets from the volunteer teachers in the parish as one prepares for the sacraments. It is first a duty of parents and godparents. It is ultimately an individual responsibility. The Church, through the parish, goes to great lengths to help with religious education, but it can only help. Each baptized person is ultimately accountable for his own religious education.

This is how that basic gift of the Spirit is made operative and more effective in a person's life. He learns to think with the "mind of the Church" by prayer and study. Thinking with the mind of the Church does not mean a person is limited to "Church approved" literature—it just means that he starts there. Certainly, if you want to know which politician's anti-poverty program best embodies the principles of social justice, you have to read the politician's program; but first you have to know what the principles of social justice *are*. Then you have to learn how to apply them to particular situations. It is a complex world, and a mature adult does not simply rely on some website telling him what the Church or a pope says. A mature adult would not be so flip about buying a new car. Nor should he be on matters that affect his growth in holiness or the common good of his fellow man.

No one needs to become a theologian, but everyone needs to be educated. There are no shortcuts, and no excuses are accepted in this army. The *sensus fidelium* is a gift to be appreciated, developed, and applied.

BAND-AIDS: CONFESSION AND SPIRITUAL DIRECTION

This section of our operations order tells us where to turn in case we are injured—or, better yet, for preventive measures against injury. In warfare, injuries are inevitable. The same is true for spiritual combat. Once you begin your training, you will be attacked. The more you advance in holiness, the worse the attacks will get. You will be injured: what do you do then?

Once again, we will focus on three things: prayer, the sacrament of confession, and spiritual direction. Since prayer has already been addressed, only a few more points need be made. Part of the regimen of prayer should be an annual retreat. Just as St. Francis would return to St. Claire and the Portiuncula when he was weary with the world, the spiritual warrior needs rest and retraining as well.

Humility

Pray for humility, particularly if you have been successful in your efforts to conquer your own sin or to enlighten others. One of the chief strategies of our enemy is to use the human propensity for pride against us. If you are successful, or even simply trying hard for personal holiness, you will be attacked. The bravest soldiers always draw the most fire. Our enemy is cunning; he will use pride to disarm you. Practice humility at all times.

For some of us, the routine humiliations we encounter will be enough to remind us that we are but dust and to dust we shall return (see Gen. 3:19). The enemy seeks to demoralize us so that we abandon the fight. Our response to failure ought to be, "A-ha! There must be a human at work here who is in need of more humility or we would not have had such a marvelous opportunity presented to us." Confound the enemy and help yourself at the same time.

The ability to strike a balance between humility and morbidity can be difficult. The reliance upon a spiritual director or even a regular confidant is necessary. Often an outside, objective eye looking at our concerns will allow us to see what we cannot from inside the battle. This is a fight, and there will be suffering. Unite your wounds and failures to his, and let his grace heal and strengthen you.

Confession

Just as many people fail to engage in the spiritual combat out of fear of the demands of discipleship, many who consider themselves part of God's army are still reluctant to take part in the sacrament of confession. Sometimes it is due to a bad experience in the confessional. Sometimes it is because they have "better" things to do for that half hour on Saturday afternoon. Worse yet, sometimes they don't know they need it. The excuses are legion—the name of one of the demons in the Gospels (see Mark 5:9, Luke 8:30, and Matt. 8:30).

Beneath these excuses, people are, perhaps, afraid of the judgment of their sin. They might be ashamed of what they have done or fearful of being assigned to carry out an onerous penance. Theologically (and practically), these reasons are nonsensical, but the fear of them is quite real. This is why I chose to present this sacrament as analogous to receiving battlefield first-aid from a medic or corpsman. Certainly the wounded Marine who cries out "Corpsman up!" desperately hopes the aid will come with speed—his life may depend on it. This ought to be our attitude toward the sacrament of confession, for one's spiritual life may be in grave danger as well.

This sacrament *is* a judgment of our sins and a penance will be assigned, but if that is where our focus (or our fear) lies, then we are missing the essential point. In this sacrament, Christ is himself our corpsman or medic. Just as those brave sailors or soldiers have as their sole mission to save the lives of wounded warriors, our Lord desires to heal our wounds—to carry us from the fight and make us whole. There may be pain involved, but it is a necessary pain, and it brings healing.

The sacrament of confession is a means of being brought back into friendship and communion with God. Sin harms or even kills that relationship. The sacrament of healing restores what has been forfeit by sin. Spiritual warriors will sin; this is how the enemy wounds us. Even the most skilled spiritual combatants suffer wounds. I once read that Pope St. John Paul II would receive the sacrament every three or four days. If he felt he needed a medic that often, it is a good bet we need one as often as well—even more frequently, perhaps, during Lent and Advent.

Like all sacraments, confession is a celebration. Yes, it does involve admission of guilt and subsequent correction, but it is the celebration that the good father held for his prodigal son (see Luke 15:11ff). The real question is: where does our focus lie? Do we dwell on the sin, on the correction, or on the reconciliation? The attitude of the penitent makes all the difference. If we dread this encounter with Christ, what are we afraid of? To see it as the heavenly medic rushing to our aid is a good way to begin to change our attitude.

We do have a High Priest who experienced human weakness (see Heb. 4:15). He knew we would be wounded, and he set up an aid station to treat those wounds—not only to heal our wounds, but to make us stronger. We do not leave this aid station simply patched up but made even better than before.

A Spiritual Director Is Like a Medic

Having a regular confessor and/or spiritual director is similar to having the corpsman or medic as a part of one's military unit. Because he works with the same people on a daily basis, he knows them well. He knows their strengths and weaknesses as well as their blood type. This allows him to be more invested in his care and more swiftly effective in administering it. A regular confessor would know of our spiritual strengths and weaknesses as well as our particular struggles. Because of this, he can prescribe a penance that would be most fitting to heal our sins. If we seldom enter the confessional and simply rattle off a list of sins by type and number, is it any surprise that the medicine administered is "three Our Fathers and three Hail Marys; now say the Act of Contrition"? That is not the kind of spiritual care our souls need and deserve, but often it is what we get—not because the medic is flawed but because he does not know us or the nature of our wounds.

A regular spiritual director is similar to the good squad leader who ensures his men are always well trained and cared for. He knows that the unit can be called into action without time to prepare, so he makes sure his men are always razor-sharp. A spiritual director can provide the continual training we need to be spiritually fit and ready for combat. This individual will know us well and understand what type of spiritual progress we have made. He (or she) will know what we need to make further progress in the spiritual life. A good director will have a sense of what our particular "mission" is (see Chapter 4 for a detailed presentation on the mission each Christian receives from Christ) and will understand what we need to carry out that mission.

A key difference between the squad leader and the spiritual director (and here the analogy breaks down) is that the latter will have the experience of a veteran in the spiritual combat because he has been in the same "fight" for many years. As noted previously, the spiritual combat is always ongoing within each individual soul. The good director knows this, because he has been engaged in it for many years. The one seeking direction may have just come to the realization that he is in a fight for his soul. Many more are under attack and do not know it. The reality is that we are all on the battlefield simply by the fact that we are human.

BAD GUYS: THE DEVIL AND HUMANS

Perhaps the easiest part of the spiritual combat is how one deals with the devil and his demons. Like all members of the animal kingdom, we have a built-in "flee or fight" mechanism. The problem for us rational animals is that we don't use it well. When one is faced with an actual demonic attack, the only appropriate response is to flee. The spiritual masters of the centuries are very clear on this point. Humans cannot contend with supernatural enemies. One must recognize when they are in a fight that is too much for them. When that *sensus fidelium* kicks in, and you understand that the devil is himself your adversary, you can only place yourself at the foot of the cross and ask that the blood of Christ wash over you and form a protective barrier. What humans are helpless against has already been remedied. Christ has already vanquished this foe, and as soon as we turn this fight over to him, victory is assured.

Stealth Combat

The obvious problem is that most often we do not recognize these attacks for what they are. Old Scratch has not really updated his tactics since his appearance in the book of Genesis. If only he were more obvious. Of course, being of angelic nature, he knows this: if he showed his true face, those under assault would know how to respond, and his defeat would be assured (though not necessarily immediate). So he hides and he lies.

This most cunning adversary takes great care to ensure that his attacks are not seen as attacks at all. He plans carefully so that his movements and urgings seem to be on a spectrum from "no big deal" to something that appears as a good. Some may think this belief is alarmist or hyperbole. Try this simple experiment. Pick your favorite television show—one that you enjoy but don't let the kids watch since it is on past their bedtime. As you watch the show, keep a paper and pen handy. Each time any of the characters commit a sin, jot it down. You can even prep with a listing of sins so you can simply place check marks under each one: wrath, avarice, sloth, pride, lust, envy, and gluttony.

It might even be handy to note a few examples of things that would fall into each category. Under wrath one could write: murder, physical violence, hatred, or spiteful words. As our Savior put it, "anyone who is angry with his brother has already committed murder in his heart" (Matt. 5:22). In the Sermon on the Mount, Christ saw the need to explain how people of his day missed the implication of the Covenant Law by failing to see that all of the deadly sins begin with an interior disposition before they are manifest in outward actions. So adultery really does begin with the lustful gaze toward or thought about someone of the opposite sex. As you keep score, include the commercials. Every time a scantily clad person or seductive image is used to spark interest in the product, that earns another check mark.

Each of the sins can be similarly expanded. Sloth is quite popular today. We have entire movies built around (usually male) characters who are "funny" because they are slackers. Grown men are presented as frozen adolescents who spend as much time as possible goofing off, playing video games, drinking beer, and doing as little work as possible. Check mark. Gluttony includes any consumption of a good taken to excess. Over-consumption of alcohol is the low-hanging fruit in this experiment. But don't limit your idea of gluttony to the consumption of food or drink. Anytime one consumes more of a good thing beyond what is actually needed for the end toward which the good is ordered is guilty of gluttony. Check mark.

So spend some time expanding each category before watching the show. Once your list is ready, tune in (or log on) and keep score. My guess is that you will surprised by just how many mortal sins had previously passed unnoticed or even seemed entertaining. (If you cannot think of any shows this might work with, good for you. Pick a show that is popular in the wider culture—one that everyone at work talks about. It will work). As a culture, we have become numbed to the instances of sin we see on a daily basis—because it is no big deal.

I was shaken out of my own complacency by two particular incidents. The first was spotting a copy of Mel Brooks's *Blazing Saddles* in the $5 bin at a local big-box store. I thought, "Hey, that was a funny movie, I'll take a copy home and let the older kids watch it." I turned the DVD case over and was reminded it was rated R. My next thought was, "Really?! There is no nudity or anything like that." So I thought about some of the scenes I knew from memory. "Up yours, nigger" (oops); then this dialogue: "What was your crime?" "Rape, murder, arson, and rape." "You said rape twice." "I like rape" (oops). A few more "funny" scenes came to mind, and I put the DVD down. I was shaken by just how many things I had laughed at that now struck me as wrong (even evil). So the DVD went back into the bin—although, much to my wife's chagrin, I did pull up the campfire farting scene on YouTube for the older boys. I'm not perfect by any means.

The second incident was a simple comment I read on a website when the movie *Titanic* was all the rage. A priest summarized the plot as "two young people commit mortal sin just before they die." Certainly there was more to the movie than that, but wasn't that also the central part of the story? Oops—once again, it had not occurred to me to see it from this perspective.

We live in an age where sin is not only no big deal; it's even funny or laudatory. The enemy really is on the prowl, seeking souls to devour. And most of us are blind to it. God have mercy, and St. Michael defend us in battle. Until one learns to see through the enemy's disguise, he has not completed his training. Until he is ready to flee to the cross when he encounters the enemy, he is not fit for battle.

Earthly Adversaries

So what then do we do with our human adversaries? They may be friends, family, objects of our evangelization efforts, clergy, and religious. One will always be oneself. All people are potential allies and potential enemies—some are just more obvious about into which camp they fall. Eventually we do need to sort out who is on our side and the other, but that is not the first step. The first step is to love them. God loves all the souls he has created. Love of God entails loving what he loves. It really is that simple (see John 13:34-35, 15:17).

In the first of St. John's letters, the community is dealing with the aftermath of some members having left the faith. The entire letter is devoted to sin, love, truth, and discernment. Christians must love everyone, even as they discern who is aligned with them and who against. As the letter makes clear, love is not just words and not even an attitude—it is manifest in actions or it is not real (see 1 John 3:18). Love can also be harsh. The letter calls on Christians to make judgments about others and to treat them accordingly—all under the banner of love. This is not simply the message for the community founded by the apostle John; it can be found in Matthew's Gospel as well (see Matt. 18:17).

When others are clearly a danger to growth in holiness, we must be prepared to act decisively. Jesus rebuked the religious leaders of his day. Paul and John went so far as to equate false teachers or sinners with the anti-Christ. If you find yourself faced with such a situation, having the mind of love includes serving others in humility *and* rebuking the sinner. St. Gregory Nazianzen wrote:

Choose then whichever blasphemy you prefer, my good inventor of a new theology, if indeed you are anxious at all costs to embrace a blasphemy. [76]

And shake the dust of their blasphemy from your feet (see Matt. 10:14, Luke 9:5). The spiritual warrior accepts all people as children of God *and* is willing to part company even with family members who remain mired in sin. Love of God includes being repulsed by things that are sinful. You cannot love others if you do not love yourself. Protecting yourself and those you love is an essential aspect of love.

If you do love yourself, it will (by definition) spill out into love for others. Love of self includes a determined effort to do three things:

- To root out our sins and our desire for sinful things. Remember, there is no possibility of a thing being a temptation unless we harbor some measure of desire for it.

- To remove oneself from the near occasion of sin. Be it a place, an activity or a person; the wall of separation must be built and fortified (See 2 Thess. 3:6 and 3:14-15).

- To love others, even across the wall; but do not remove the wall. The goal is *not* to break down the wall but to win others to the correct side of it.

76. Gregory Nazianzen, *Third Oration*, ch. X.

Finally, when trying to discern in which camp you or others are currently, remember that one can always move from one side of the fight to the other. Be fearful, because moving from Christ's camp to the enemy's can be subtle and (initially) unnoticed. Be hopeful, because change is possible for as long as one draws breath. Be vigilant for the same reasons.

5

COMMAND AND
SIGNAL

THE COMMAND AND SIGNAL PARAGRAPH PROVIDES
THE IDENTIFICATION AND MISSION OF A UNIT'S
HIGHER HEADQUARTERS AS WELL AS ANY ADJACENT
OR SUPPORTING UNITS. IT SPECIFIES THE RE-
LATIONSHIPS BETWEEN PARTICIPATING UNITS AND
WHICH UNITS ARE RESPONSIBLE FOR WHAT PARTS
OF THE OPERATION.

All military units have something called a "chain of command." This is the designation of which commanders
are in charge from the commander-in-chief down to the individual unit. Often there are portraits in a unit's headquarters
of each individual, reminding all passersby who is in the chain
of command. Just as often, there are also pictures of people
who are not technically in the chain of command but occupy
important positions.

For example, the sergeants major (senior enlisted member
of a unit) are included, along with each commanding officer. Sergeants major are not commanders, but no unit can
function well without them. Also, the vast majority of most
combat units are enlisted men, and they don't really want to
deal with officers unless absolutely necessary.

PRELIMINARY DIFFICULTIES

This may sound complex, but it is really quite simple. For an infantry battalion, typically there would be: the U.S. president, the commandant of the Marine Corps, the MEF (Marine Expeditionary Force) commanding general, the division commanding general, the regimental commander, and the battalion commander.

For the modern spiritual soldier, the chain of command is even simpler, and I will include one individual who is not in the chain of command but is necessary for its effective functioning. For most of us it is: the pope, the local bishop, one's parish priest, and, finally, one's family. The parish priest is not technically in the chain of command, but we will see shortly why he is included.

Before looking at the mission and function of each member of the chain of command, it is necessary to address a few common objections one may encounter about today's Church. These may be attitudes held by those whom one hopes to evangelize, or attitudes the reader may hold.

Distrust of Church Hierarchy

First among these is a distrust of the Church hierarchy. Because of the early-twenty-first-century priest sex-abuse crisis, many people—Catholics and non-Catholics—developed a distrust of the bishops and (perhaps) the pope. Often this is expressed vaguely (at least among Catholics). People seem to like Pope Francis but don't like "the Vatican." Many are distrustful of "the bishops," but their own guy is okay (it is all those *other* ones who are the problem).

There are valid reasons for this attitude. There are also silly ones and damaging ones. How one addresses the attitude depends on what reasons give rise to it. Most people have a justifiable lack of enthusiasm for any bureaucracy. We all dread the annual visit to the DMV, although we may harbor no ill will toward anyone we know who works there. It seems that even popes have the same attitude toward bureaucracies. One popular anecdote about Pope John XXIII (reigned 1958-1963) makes this clear: when asked how many people work in the Vatican, he is said to have answered, "About half of them." This level of skepticism of "the Vatican" (or "the chancery") is harmless.

A silly reason for distrust would be that "the bishops" did or did not do (fill in the blank). This is silly because "the bishops" as a group have no real authority. The United States Conference of Catholic Bishops (USCCB) is an administrative body. Nothing they do or say as a group has any weight until one's local bishop gives it the weight of his office. One can lament some of this group's actions or statements (I find the documents "Always Our Children" and "Built of Living Stones" particularly troubling), but until the local bishop decides to make the USCCB policy/statement his own, it means nothing.

More serious problems came to light because of the sex-abuse crisis. But even here, objections may still be misguided. "The bishops" did not hide or transfer known molesters; individual bishops did. To distrust the episcopacy as a whole because of the actions of a few individuals is a knee-jerk reaction. To the extent that they have not been held accountable, it remains a difficulty—but, as we will see, one that is more complex than most people realize. Justice will always be served (eventually), but it may not be in the manner one desires.

Is a Hierarchy Necessary?

Some people believe a hierarchy is superfluous. They might ask why we even need a pope or a bishop when we can go directly to God. This attitude can be harmless or dangerous, depending on what such an attitude actually means.

Not only can any individual "go directly to God," he *should*—daily (if not more frequently). We call this prayer, and it is an integral part of the ongoing training for modern spiritual combat. God desires a personal relationship of love with every soul he has created. It is difficult to have a relationship with anyone unless we are in close and regular contact with him or her. The same applies to our relationship with God: we need to in an ongoing and regular series of conversations with him. We need to love him directly and personally.[77]

Does this mean that the Church's hierarchy is superfluous? Absolutely not. St. John explains that if we love God, we will keep his commands (see John 14:15). Jesus said whoever listens to his disciples is actually hearing his voice and the voice of his Father (see Luke 10:16). The Church that Jesus founded was (and remains) a hierarchical organization that was given (and retains) his authority.

It was popular in the 1970s to say that Jesus came to build a kingdom on Earth, not to start a Church. There are still many in the Church who learned that lesson (and cannot seem to move beyond it), so this attitude is still encountered today. It is silly and dangerous.

Silly because any objective reading of Scripture makes it

---

77. In the Marines, there is a procedure called "Request Mast" (and the other services have an equivalent). This allows any individual Marine to speak directly to his commanding officer if he has a situation that warrants such action. Though good leadership demands such a provision; it is not the way 99 percent of problems are handled.

quite clear that Jesus came to build a kingdom *and* to found a Church. More importantly, he meant for that kingdom to be built by his Church and never apart from it. It is also silly because any human organization needs some type of structure. There are no examples of an effective human organization that does not have some form of governance structure.[78]

This attitude is dangerous to the extent that it leads people to see their relationship with God as only existing between themselves and God. As in most things Catholic, it is a "both/and" rather than an "either/or" thing. In this case, the either/or view has serious consequences. Pope Benedict XVI (in *Spe Salvi*, "Saved in Hope") pointed out that salvation itself is always a communal effect of Christ. We are each personally (but not individually) saved by the grace of Christ. We are always (and only) saved as members of that mystical body of Christ of which St. Paul speaks so often.

If a person sees faith as a relationship between himself and God *alone*; he is missing an essential truth about salvation. One must have a personal relationship of love with God that includes a love of others. If the person loves God, he must love what/whom God loves. And what/whom God loves is all of creation and everybody.

Obedience

So the hierarchy is necessary; but what about obedience? Recall what was said about the "center of gravity" earlier. The demands of discipleship seem to be a key problem for

78. This is also an application of one of the principles of social justice called subsidiarity. Issues are to be addressed at the local or lowest level possible that encompasses those who are concerned, and higher levels of organization (of society) have an obligation to support and empower the lower levels.

the New Evangelization. This may manifest itself in the belief that one may have loving relationship with God without being obedient to "the hierarchy." But Scripture passages noted above (and many others) about the necessity of the Church apply here as well. Obedience to Jesus *is* obedience to the hierarchy, because he explicitly said so and arranged it that way. This is the *normal* way of holiness.

Normal in this sense means the way it works, by design, for the vast majority of people. Of course, God can grant faith and salvation to a soul in any manner he chooses. Part of what it means to be God is that he can do whatever he wills to do. Part of being human (in general) and a believer (in particular) is not to tell God what he can or cannot do. Christ gave his authority to his apostles (see John 20:22-23). He founded a Church meant to last for all time. So obedience to the Church he started is really obedience to him. And obedience to him (and his Church) is the sure sign of love of him.

It really is that simple. It is also a real difficulty. Like any human institution, the Church is not perfect; nothing is perfect outside of God and heaven. Despite the ongoing activity and presence of the Holy Spirit and of Christ himself, the Church is still human. It has inherited the mission of the One who was both human and divine; it is both human and divine. Because of the ongoing activity and presence of the Holy Spirit and of Christ himself, the Church has an authority that requires our obedience because it is divine; but not a blind obedience, because it is human. Just as it is a both/and (not an either/or), it is a matter of balance.

The final dangerous problem of the "I can go directly to God" attitude is that we humans are masters at deceiving ourselves. It can be very difficult to know when I am following God's will for me and when I am following the desires of my own ego. It is rare (if not unknown) that God wants us to have a Mercedes-Benz; but it is quite easy for us to think he does. As we saw in our examination of spiritual directors in the previous chapter, we need an outsider's objective eye to help us discern when God is speaking to us and when that voice we hear is simply the echo of our ego. We need at least one trusted member of the mystical body of Christ—and we can't have one part without having the whole thing.

It gets worse—the enemy is at work here. Asymmetrical warfare comes into play where the devil seeks to convince us that the suggestion we hear in our heart is not his voice but God's. Human history has no shortage of instances where people who thought they were doing God's will when actually accomplishing the schemes of the Evil One. This is such a clear and present danger that St. John of the Cross warned his fellow Carmelites to treat any mystical experience they had as being instigated by the devil until they had clearly been able to discern otherwise. Most of us will not be subject to the attacks that St. John of the Cross experienced. The enemy saves his most devastating attacks for the boldest spiritual warriors. But all who take up the spiritual combat will be attacked.

THE CHAIN OF COMMAND

As we examine the chain of command, it is important to note that persons or personalities are not important. Although I may have preferred a commandant who was from an infantry background, if he was a pilot, he was still my commandant. We may like (or dislike) a particular pope or bishop, but that is without any bearing. The office, not the person, is what counts. The alternative is to develop a cult of personality. Or worse.

Recall Jesus' words about the faith of the centurion in Capernaum (see Matt. 8:5-13). That Roman soldier understood the concept. Just as he was a man under obedience, so are we. If we are obedient only to a pope, bishop, or priest when we like them (or agree with them), then we are really following our own desires. We make ourselves rather than God the measure of our faith. Instead of a cult of personality, we have set up a cult of narcissism.

Because of the centurion's act of faith, Jesus healed his servant. More importantly, he was moved to comment that faithful obedience was one of the keys to eternal life. Many of the pious Jews in Israel, who followed the Law and the leaders of their day, would be cast out of the kingdom. The centurion would be welcomed. This is why we make that Roman soldier's words our own in the Mass ("Lord, I am not worthy that you should enter under my roof"). The warrior in spiritual combat is under obedience, particularly when he does not fully understand; more so when he disagrees.

The Pope

Jesus founded his Church on the disciple whom he named "the Rock." St. Peter, despite all his personal failings, was the one identified by the Father to lead the early Church. He was also called aside by the risen Christ and told that it was he who must strengthen the other apostles and care for the entire Church (see John 21:15-19). At Rome, Peter passed his authority to Linus. As we hear in the first Eucharistic prayer, the next in line was Cletus, then Clement. This prayer draws on the writings of the Bishop of Lyons, St. Irenaeus. In his book *Against Heresies* (and there were many in his day; second-century A.D.), he addresses papal succession and Church authority in general, because it was under attack.[79] St. Irenaeus

79. Irenaeus of Lyon, *Against Heresies*, book 3, § 3.

states that the same level of detail could be supplied for any local church but that it was most important to do so for the Church of Rome, since it was the head of all the churches.

History makes clear that not every pope is a saint. The grace of ordination and the charism of elevation to the papacy are powerful but not a panacea. But the office and the authority entrusted to it by God himself cannot be changed and demand our allegiance. We may have a particular attraction to or coldness toward any particular pope, but he is our "commanding general" once we are baptized into service.

One of the titles for the pope is "Vicar of Christ." A vicar is a person who is the personal representative of a ruler when that ruler cannot be present. The vicar carries the same authority as the absent ruler. Jesus said he had received all authority in heaven and Earth from his Father (see Matt. 28:18). He bestowed that same authority on St. Peter (see Matt. 16:19) and the other apostles (see Matt. 18:18). To love God is to follow his commands. One can do so only by following those to whom he has entrusted his Church.

The Bishop

Next in our chain of command is the bishop of our own local Church.[80] One of the strong areas of emphasis at the Second Vatican Council was on the role and authority of the individual bishop. Each bishop is a successor to the apostles and carries the same authority given to them. It may not be possible to trace the chain of succession for today's bishops

---

80. Much of what follows about the bishop is technically true of what canon law calls the "local ordinary" and not necessarily of every bishop. Since for most readers these terms appear to be interchangeable, I will not address the differences and simply use "bishop."

as easily as was done by St. Irenaeus. The passing of eighteen more centuries (and human shenanigans) have complicated the process. But the office retains the authority necessary for it to be effective in accomplishing its mission: the salvation of souls.

Seeing Church authority in this way is essential. We have seen that it is the authority handed on by God incarnate. But it is authority with a purpose, not authority for its own sake. Even if it has been exercised in that way in the past (and it has), that was an aberration that does not negate the proper role of that authority. Historical (or current) abuses undermine authority but do not cancel it out. People shy away from the demands of discipleship. Americans chafe under any form of authority. But if we can see it as it truly is—authority directed toward the mission of the Redeemer—it becomes easier to submit to it.

Each bishop (and others, as we will see) is given the responsibility for the souls entrusted to him. He is to be shepherd to these souls and do all in his power to get them to heaven. During the Last Supper, Jesus prayed to his Father for his disciples. He noted in that prayer that he had not lost any of those the Father had given him (see John 17:12).

Think for a minute about the effect this part of the prayer had on the apostles. Even if was not clear at the moment the words were spoken, it soon became clear and has been central to the understanding of the role of the bishop ever since. Jesus is going to pass his authority and his Church into their care. He prays to his Father to help prepare them for this responsibility. In the course of that prayer he points out that he has not lost a single one whom he was supposed to lead. The clear implication is this: that they must do as he did and not lose those entrusted to them.

I know that during my active duty time, if my commanding officer had done such a thing, I would clearly understand he was telling me: "Now if you mess this up, I'll have your a##!" That kind of message has a unique kind of urgency.

Of course, our Lord and Savior was/is a far better leader than any human commanding officer. Nonetheless, the Church has understood these words in a similar manner. Those who are charged with the responsibility for souls will be called to account for how they handled those souls. Did they do all in their power to ensure none were lost? Personally, I would not want to be at the Pearly Gates and be asked by St. Peter to account for all the souls of a diocese.

Each of us will be asked to account for the care we took of our own soul. Some are asked about their care for the souls of others, bishops more so than the rest of us. So, if your bishop does not seem to be quite hard enough on dissenters, remember that he must do all he can to help them. And he cannot help those who turn away from him and refuse to listen. Knowing that he will be asked if he did all he could, he will err on the side of salvation (both his own and the dissenters').

Since I have mentioned that balance is central to our training for service as a modern knight, a little balance is needed here. Each individual is responsible for the fate of his own eternal soul. Others have some share in that responsibility, but ultimately it is the individual who stands before the Just Judge. The bishop is responsible for what he can do—not for the outcome of those efforts. The individual soul owns the outcome.

Before we turn to the role of the priest, there are a few words about balance I need to include for any clergy reading this book. In the effort to save sinners by not being too harsh with them, consider the effect this has on those of the faithful who are already filling the pews and working toward holiness. It can dishearten for one working hard to live the demands of discipleship to see publicly acknowledged sinners being treated with "kid gloves."

My experience as a commander provides a useful analogy. One of the tasks of a good commander is to keep his best warriors motivated. It is natural for any leader to spend 80 percent of his time with 20 percent of his people—and often these are the "problem children" who demand (and deserve) a leader's attention. Just don't allow yourself to be so focused on them that you neglect those who are not so needy.

The Priest

Let us turn now to that person we included in the chain of command who is not (technically) a commander: the parish priest.[81] Strictly speaking, he is an extension of the bishop and derives his authority from him. In the Marines, a platoon commander was not legally a commanding officer—he did not have the same authority under the Uniform Code of Military Justice that a commander had. But to the members of his platoon, this was a distinction without a difference. The same understanding applies here. For most people, the parish priest is the "face" of the Church and its authority; this is why he is included in our chain of command.

For the vast majority of Catholics, the priest (and the parish) are the center of the experience of being part of the mystical body of Christ. It is in this gathering and from this man that they receive the sacraments, hear the gospel, and experience the life of the Church. This is where most everything that matters happens. This gives rise to a danger that can

---

81. Again, I am consciously ignoring canon law distinctions between pastors, parochial vicars, parochial administrators, and generic "priests." They are important distinctions; but not to this book's intended audience.

be almost as damaging as failure to recognize due authority.

The opposite can happen at the parish level where too much authority is given. The counterpart (or analog) to seeing the hierarchy as superfluous is seeing the parish as the full extent of the mystical body of Christ. It is an error to believe the individual alone before God needs no Church, and so is seeing "the people of God" as simply my little slice of it in the local parish.[82] In a similar fashion, the priest who is the center of the ministry in the parish can become the center of attention. This may be something the priest encourages or something bestowed on him by his parishioners despite his best efforts against it. A sure sign that a cult of personality has developed around a priest is the level of outcry when his assignment is changed. If people are writing to the bishop to explain why Fr. So-and-So cannot possibly be moved, there is a problem. He, rather than Christ, has become the center of the life of the parish. This is why canon law expects that priests will be reassigned on a regular and recurring basis—to guard against this very real (and very natural human) tendency.

Respect your priests, but don't idolize them. They are your brothers and your allies, so listen to them. They are human, so correct or question them when necessary.

The Family

The next-to-last level in our chain of command is the family. Pope St. John Paul II called attention to the importance of the Christian family. He brought back into use the term "domestic Church" to emphasize that the family is the original and indispensable Church in miniature. It is here that people

---

82. The phrases "people of God" and "Church" are two ways of designating the same reality. Some today ignore the fact that the hierarchy is also a part of that "people."

learn what the word *love* means. His apostolic exhortation *Familiaris Consortio* (1981) is required reading for all members of this outfit.

In this letter, our past Holy Father laid out God's vision for the human family. It is the cradle of not only the Church but of civilization in general. Leadership, humility, justice, and all other aspects of love are meant to be learned in this environment. This is what God created human families to be. Certainly, not all families embody this vision, and none do so perfectly. But until one encounters this vision, there is no possibility of striving for it. St. John Paul was fond of saying, "Family, become what you are." He did this to acknowledge that we fall short of the mark and to inspire us to keep working toward it. In his mind, if one encounters God's vision—if one can be given a glimpse of the God's-eye point of view—one can make progress toward that vision. We can work toward a goal only if we understand what that goal is.

The future of the Church, the culture, and all of society passes by way of the family. It is in that setting one learns what it means to be human, an adult, a man or a woman, and a disciple. The human family truly is the cradle of civilization. Taking this responsibility with the gravity it deserves is essential.

The Self

The last level of our chain of command is the self. Self is listed last because the command and signal section of an operations order is hierarchical. In reality, the self is primary. Recall Balthasar's description of the book of Revelation, where the battle between good and evil is waged simultaneously on multiple levels. Until the interior battle is engaged, one cannot move on to other fields of battle.

Prayer is the means of the interior combat, as well as preparation for the battle on other levels. It is truly a three-dimensional ongoing struggle. The battle will not end on any of the three levels during your lifetime. Begin the interior and move outward while never ceasing the interior operation. The more successful you are, the more of the enemy's attention you draw. He will fight you on all levels using his asymmetric approach.

We have already covered some of this ground. The individual soul is judged either worthy of heaven (via purgatory for most of us) or hell. At one point we will stand alone before the Just Judge. Although we stand alone, we do not stand in solitude. At that moment, just as in our earthly life, we will be surrounded by the "cloud of witnesses" (Heb. 12:1). They will join with the Christ in his judgment, because they are totally conformed to his will. They will rejoice or weep, because they will know to what degree we accepted their help in the battle. We are never alone in life or in death.

But we are ultimately responsible for ourselves. When Shakespeare wrote "to thine own self be true," he was (perhaps inadvertently) voicing a theological truth. To be true to yourself can have two divergent meanings. It can mean being true to our nature as image and likeness of God. It can also mean seeing yourself as the rugged individual and sole measure of goodness, truth, and beauty. This was the problem reflected in the book of Genesis, and it is the same problem today.

In the Army, every soldier is responsible for keeping himself and his gear ready for battle. In spiritual combat, every soldier is responsible for making sure he is fit for battle. Each soldier has entire commands dedicated to providing him with the equipment and training he needs. The entire mystical body of Christ (and the angels) stand ready to provide the Christian soldier with all he needs. God himself is ever present to assist us as well. As St. Augustine wrote in his *Confessions*, God was closer to him than he was to himself.

In the final analysis, everything comes down to the individual. Success in combat can depend on one action by one soldier. Once the fighting gets hot, the generals must sit back and watch, entirely dependent on the actions of the lance corporals doing the fighting. Spiritual combat is no different. Each person has a mission to perform, and only that person can perform it. The battle is at hand; each of us must decide what part he will play in it.

About the Author

Dan McGuire, Ph.D., is associate professor of theology and ministry at the University of Great Falls, Montana. Prior to becoming a theology professor, he served for twenty years as an infantry officer in the Marines. His special interest is fundamental theology—in particular, helping Catholics rediscover the philosophical underpinnings of the Faith. A father of eight, Dan lives in Great Falls with his wife and younger children.

CPSIA information can be obtained
at www.ICGtesting.com
Printed in the USA
BVHW031624120920
588315BV00003BA/12